America Online® 7.0
FOR
DUMMIES®
QUICK REFERENCE

by Jennifer Kaufeld

Hungry Minds™

Best-Selling Books • Digital Downloads • e-Books • Answer Networks
e-Newsletters • Branded Web Sites • e-Learning

New York, NY ◆ Cleveland, OH ◆ Indianapolis, IN

American Online® 7.0 For Dummies® Quick Reference

Published by
Hungry Minds, Inc.
909 Third Avenue
New York, NY 10022
www.hungryminds.com
www.dummies.com

Library of Congress Control Number: 2001093696

ISBN: 0-7645-1625-6

Printed in the United States of America

10 9 8 7 6 5 4 3 2 1

1O/RU/RR/QR/IN

Distributed in the United States by Hungry Minds, Inc.

Distributed by CDG Books Canada Inc. for Canada; by Transworld Publishers Limited in the United Kingdom; by IDG Norge Books for Norway; by IDG Sweden Books for Sweden; by IDG Books Australia Publishing Corporation Pty. Ltd. for Australia and New Zealand; by TransQuest Publishers Pte Ltd. for Singapore, Malaysia, Thailand, Indonesia, and Hong Kong; by Gotop Information Inc. for Taiwan; by ICG Muse, Inc. for Japan; by Intersoft for South Africa; by Eyrolles for France; by International Thomson Publishing for Germany, Austria and Switzerland; by Distribuidora Cuspide for Argentina; by LR International for Brazil; by Galileo Libros for Chile; by Ediciones ZETA S.C.R. Ltda. for Peru; by WS Computer Publishing Corporation, Inc., for the Philippines; by Contemporanea de Ediciones for Venezuela; by Express Computer Distributors for the Caribbean and West Indies; by Micronesia Media Distributor, Inc. for Micronesia; by Chips Computadoras S.A. de C.V. for Mexico; by Editorial Norma de Panama S.A. for Panama; by American Bookshops for Finland.

For general information on Hungry Minds' products and services please contact our Customer Care Department within the U.S. at 800-762-2974, outside the U.S. at 317-572-3993 or fax 317-572-4002.

For sales inquiries and reseller information, including discounts, premium and bulk quantity sales, and foreign-language translations, please contact our Customer Care Department at 800-434-3422, fax 317-572-4002, or write to Hungry Minds, Inc., Attn: Customer Care Department, 10475 Crosspoint Boulevard, Indianapolis, IN 46256.

For information on licensing foreign or domestic rights, please contact our Sub-Rights Customer Care Department at 212-884-5000.

For information on using Hungry Minds' products and services in the classroom or for ordering examination copies, please contact our Educational Sales Department at 800-434-2086 or fax 317-572-4005.

For press review copies, author interviews, or other publicity information, please contact our Public Relations Department at 317-572-3168 or fax 317-572-4168.

For authorization to photocopy items for corporate, personal, or educational use, please contact Copyright Clearance Center, 222 Rosewood Drive, Danvers, MA 01923, or fax 978-750-4470.

Hungry Minds is a trademark of Hungry Minds, Inc.

About the Author

Jennifer Kaufeld spends most waking hours in front of the computer, writing about technology or reviewing educational software for homeschoolers and home-education journals. Any free time finds her researching and re-creating Victorian and pre-1950s needlework, speaking at home education conventions about the educational use of computers and software, or presiding over the Greek and English lessons in the family homeschool. Writing several America Online books hasn't deterred her from the fun of tracking down new online areas and features. Look for her lurking around the system under the screen name JSKaufeld.

Dedication

To J.B. and the Baylet, for patiently wondering when Mom would take a break from writing and make some dinner.

Author's Acknowledgments

As with any project, there are a zillion people who helped along the way. At Hungry Minds, Inc., my Project Editor, Nicole Haims, deserves a great big box of chocolate Popsicles for a job well done — as we all know, nothing tops chocolate. This was our second project together, and we both survived admirably. Thanks for making it easy — I look forward to creating another book with you in the future.

My Copy Editor, Teresa Artman, gets all kinds of kudos for stepping into the project and finishing the last minute details. Wearing two hats is never an easy task, but you did a great job! Thanks for all your hard work and your willingness to fill in where needed.

My Technical Editor, Lee Musick, painstakingly checked the chapters to ensure their correctness. Thanks, Lee.

At AOL-land in Virginia, special thanks go to John, Adam, Reggie, and Travis, who collectively know more secret stuff about AOL than the CIA knows about Russia. Without you guys, this book just wouldn't have happened.

As always, a huge thank you to my husband John, who patiently played tag team with me (while trying to finish his own AOL book) so that between us we managed to keep the household running and deadlines mostly intact.

Finally, thanks to all my friends in the online world who threw in tips, suggestions, and mental support. Thanks particularly to Carol, Cheryl, Kathi, Lisa, Matt, Rhonda, and everyone else. You help keep me sane.

Publisher's Acknowledgments

We're proud of this book; please send us your comments through our Hungry Minds Online Registration Form located at www.dummies.com.

Some of the people who helped bring this book to market include the following:

Acquisitions, Editorial, and Media Development

Senior Project Editor: Nicole Haims

Senior Acquisitions Editor: Steven H. Hayes

Copy Editor: Teresa Artman

Technical Editor: Lee Musick

Editorial Manager: Leah Cameron

Media Development Manager: Laura VanWinkle

Media Development Supervisor: Richard Graves

Editorial Assistant: Jean Rogers

Production

Project Coordinator: Maridee Ennis

Layout and Graphics: Gabrielle McCann, Jill Piscitelli, Jacque Schneider, Betty Schulte, Julie Trippetti

Proofreaders: Laura Albert, Andy Hollandbeck, Susan Moritz, Marianne Santy, TECHBOOKS Production Services

Indexer: TECHBOOKS Production Services

General and Administrative

Hungry Minds Publishing Group: Richard Swadley, Senior Vice President and Publisher; Mary Bednarek, Vice President and Publisher, Networking; Joseph Wikert, Vice President and Publisher, Web Development Group; Mary C. Corder, Editorial Director, Dummies Technology; Andy Cummings, Publishing Director, Dummies Technology; Barry Pruett, Publishing Director, Visual/Graphic Design

Hungry Minds Manufacturing: Ivor Parker, Vice President, Manufacturing

Hungry Minds Marketing: John Helmus, Assistant Vice President, Director of Marketing

Hungry Minds Production for Branded Press: Debbie Stailey, Production Director

Hungry Minds Sales: Michael Violano, Vice President, International Sales and Sub Rights

Contents at a Glance

The Big Picture: America Online BP-1

Part I: Personalizing Your Corner of the World 1

Part II: Navigating Here, There, and Everywhere 25

Part III: Chatting with Everyone 37

Part IV: IM Your Buddy, Locate Your Pal 53

Part V: Expressing Yourself with E-Mail 67

Part VI: Diving into Discussion Boards 95

Part VII: Saving and Sharing Pictures Online.....................107

Part VIII: Downloading, Logging, Printing, and Saving 121

Part IX: Exploring the Internet 133

Part X: Taking AOL on the Road 153

Part XI: Solving Problems and Finding Help 165

Appendix A: Places of Our Hearts.......................................175

Appendix B: Clicking through the Channels 185

Glossary: Tech Talk..195

Index 201

Table of Contents

The Big Picture: America Online BP-1

What You See: The America Online Welcome Window BP-2
What You See: Dialog Boxes BP-4
Toolbar Table BP-6
The Basics: Signing On...BP-7
The Basics: Using Keywords to Open Online Areas BP-8
The Basics: Using My Places to Locate Favorite Areas.......BP-9
The Basics: Getting Online Help BP-10
The Basics: Signing Off America Online BP-11
What You Can Do: Read Today's Headlines BP-12
What You Can Do: Send an E-Mail Message BP-13
What You Can Do: Research a Topic on the Web................BP-14

Part 1: Personalizing Your Corner of the World 1

Bringing the News to Your Mailbox 2
Changing Your Member Profile....................................2
Changing Your Password...2
Changing Your Preferences 3
   Association..4
   Auto AOL 4
   Chat 5
   Download 5
   Filing Cabinet 5
   Font, Text & Graphics 5
   Internet Properties (WWW).....................................6
   Mail 7
   Marketing 7
   Multimedia 8
   Passwords 8
   Privacy 9
   Spelling 9
   Toolbar & Sound 9
Creating a Screen Name...10
Deleting a Screen Name 12
Limiting Your Child's Online Access 12
Making Your Member Profile 13
My Calendar 14
My News..17
Parental Controls 19
   Setting Up a General Parental Controls 20
   Setting Up Custom Controls 21
Restoring a Screen Name...22

Part II: Navigating Here, There, and Everywhere 25

Adding Something to Your Favorite Places List 26
Browsing the Channels 26
Building Your Own HotKeys List 27
Changing Something in the Favorite Places List 28
Deleting Items from the Favorite Places List 29
Favorite Places 30
Finding Almost Anything on America Online 30
Flipping between Windows 31
Getting a List of Keywords 31
Going to a Favorite Place..32
Locating Keywords..33
Organizing Favorite Places 33
Remembering Your Favorite Online Spots 34
Selecting My Places 34
Using a Keyword 36

Part III: Chatting with Everyone 37

Chats Run by AOL Protocol 38
Chat Room Fonts and Formatting 38
Chatting on AOL 38
Creating a Buddy Chat Room 39
Creating a Member Chat Room 39
Creating a Private Chat Room..40
Creating a Profile 41
Expressing Yourself in a Chat Room 41
Finding Chat Rooms 42
Finding Your Favorite Community 43
Getting Help in a Chat Room..44
Going to a Friend's Chat Room 44
Locating Someone on America Online 46
People Connection 46
Playing Sounds in a Chat Room 47
Reading Someone's Profile 47
Right-Clicking in Chat Rooms 48
Role-Playing Chat Rooms 48
Rolling Dice in a Chat Room 49
Using a Profile 49
Using Chat Rooms Safely..49
  Chat room Notify AOL button 50
  General chat room dos and don'ts 50
  Ignoring someone in a chat room 51
  Reporting problems in a chat room 51

Part IV: IM Your Buddy, Locate Your Pal 53

Adding a Buddy to Your Buddy List.............................54
Adding a Buddy to Your Address Book........................54
Adding Links to Instant Messages 54
Buddy Lists 55
Changing a Buddy List Group....................................56
Creating and Using Away Messages...........................56
   Creating an Away Message....................................56
   Using an Away Message 57
Creating a Buddy Chat Room 57
Creating a Buddy List Group......................................59
Deleting a Buddy List Group 59
Formatting Instant Messages 60
Getting Info about Your Buddies 60
Instant Messages (IMs) 61
Reading Someone's Profile from the IM Window......61
Receiving Instant Messages 61
Reporting Problems in an Instant Message 62
   Someone asks for your password or credit card 62
   Someone acts generally obnoxious and annoying....63
Searching the Member Directory................................63
Sending Instant Messages 65
Setting Buddy List Preferences..................................65

Part V: Expressing Yourself with E-Mail 67

AOL Address Book 68
   Adding an Address Book entry 68
   Addressing e-mail with the Address Book..............69
   Changing or deleting an Address Book entry 70
Attaching a File to an E-Mail Message 70
Automatic AOL 72
Checking E-Mail Status...74
Copying Others with CC/BCC 75
Creating an E-Mail Signature File 76
Dealing with Undeliverable E-Mail 77
Deleting an E-Mail Message......................................77
Dropping a Signature into Your E-Mail 78
E-Mail Etiquette...80
Expressing Yourself in E-Mail 80
   Emoticons {*}, ;) 80
   Keyboard shorthand...81
Formatting E-Mail 82
Reading E-Mail...84
   Reading e-mail offline 84
   Reading e-mail online 84

Receiving Official AOL Mail..85
Receiving an Attached File in an E-Mail Message 85
Replying to an E-Mail Message 86
Saving Individual E-Mail Messages..87
Sending E-Mail...87
    Sending an e-mail greeting card 87
    Sending e-mail to AOL members..88
    Sending e-mail to several addresses......................................88
    Sending e-mail to people on the Internet..............................89
Setting Your E-Mail Preferences 89
Sharing Favorite Places in an E-Mail 89
Sorting E-Mail 90
Undeleting an E-Mail Message 90
Unsending E-Mail 91
Using Automatic AOL..91
Using a Signature in E-Mail 91
What's Your E-Mail Address? 92
Writing an E-Mail Message..92
    Writing an e-mail message offline 92
    Writing an e-mail message online 93
    Writing e-mail with the Address Book 94

Part VI: Diving into Discussion Boards........95

Checking for New Discussion Board Messages 96
Creating a Private Discussion Area 97
Creating a Public Discussion Area 99
Discussion Boards 100
Groups@AOL...101
Inviting a Friend to Join Your Group 101
Joining a Friend's Private Discussion Group 102
Posting a Reply to a Discussion Board 102
Reading a Discussion Board Message 104
Replying to a Discussion Board via E-Mail 105

Part VII: Saving and Sharing Pictures Online 107

Changing Your Online Album 108
Creating Albums 109
    Creating albums from your pictures....................................109
    Creating albums from Buddy Albums you receive............111
Developing You've Got Pictures 112
Receiving Buddy Albums...113
Saving Your Pictures Online 115
    Saving an entire roll of film 115
    Saving new pictures one by one 115
Sharing the Buddy Albums You Create 115
Using You've Got Pictures with Digital Photos.......................117
You've Got Pictures 119

Part VIII: Downloading, Logging, Printing, and Saving 121

Checking File Descriptions 122
Choosing Where to Store Files to Download 122
Downloading Files from E-Mail Messages 122
Downloading Files Later (The Download Manager) 123
Downloading Files Right Now 124
Finding Files to Download 126
Logging Chats, IMs, and Sessions.......................................126
Printing...128
Saving Text from a Window..128
Seeing Which Files You've Already Downloaded 129
Uploading Files 129
ZIP Files 131

Part IX: Exploring the Internet..................... 133

E-Mail 134
File Transfer Protocol (FTP) 134
  Downloading files from FTP sites 135
  Uploading to FTP sites 136
  Using a particular FTP site...137
Mailing Lists 138
Newsgroups..139
  Posting messages to a newsgroup 140
  Reading newsgroups online...140
  Reading newsgroups offline...141
  Remembering a newsgroup with Favorite Places..............143
  Replying to a newsgroup posting 144
  Subscribing to a newsgroup 144
  Searching for a particular topic 145
  Browsing through the lists..146
  Unsubscribing from a newsgroup......................................146
Search Systems on the Net 147
Winsock Applications and AOL 147
World Wide Web Adventures 148
  Building a home page 149
  Making your own Web page...149
  Going to a specific Web site...150
  Using Microsoft Internet Explorer with AOL....................151
  Using Netscape Navigator with AOL 151
  Remembering a site through Favorite Places 152
  Visiting friends at AOL Hometown 152

Part X: Taking AOL on the Road 153

Accessing Your Mail by Phone 154
Changing a Location...154

Connecting from a Hotel 155
Creating a Location 155
Creating a Location with Expert Add....................158
Deleting a Location..160
Finding a New Local Access Number.......................160
Making Location Entries 162
Signing On through the Internet...............................162
Signing On through Someone Else's Computer 163

Part XI: Solving Problems and Finding Help 165

Adding Your Own Two Cents Worth 166
AOL Help 166
AOL Tray Icon 167
Billing Problems 168
Calling America Online for Help 169
Finding a Lost Window 169
Free Help from Other Members 169
Freeing Up Some Virtual Space...............................170
    Reducing the Personal Filing Cabinet.............170
    Purge cache: AOL Tray icon 171
Get Help Now 172
Host Not Responding 172
Lost Carrier 173
World Wide Web Page Won't Load...........................174

Appendix A: Places of Our Hearts 175

Ages & Stages 176
AOL Hometown..176
Billing Center...176
Build Your Web Page 177
Celebrities 177
Conspiracies and UFOs 177
Daily Byte...178
Dilbert Zone...178
Evening Essentials 178
Explore 179
Food & Recipes 179
Learning Network 179
Games..180
History 180
Homeschooling..180
Homework Help 180
International 181
My News..181
The New York Times on AOL 181
Notify AOL 182

O2 Simplify...182
Radio@AOL 182
Science..183
What's New 183
Where Were You When 183
Who Am I? 184
Your Favorite Team 184

Appendix B: Clicking through the Channels 185

Welcome..186
Autos 186
Careers & Work..186
Computer Center 187
Entertainment 187
Games..188
Health 188
House & Home 189
International 189
Kids Only 190
Local Guide 190
Music 191
News 191
Parenting 191
Personal Finance 192
Research & Learn 192
Shopping 193
Sports..193
Teens 193
Travel 194
Women 194

Glossary: Tech Talk..................................... 195

Index 201

America Online

Before venturing into the Great Unknown, the pilot checks her aircraft, the captain walks his ship, and the race-car driver sits in an impossible yoga position while the crew tests the car (race car drivers are pretty odd sometimes). Likewise, you need to check out your vessel — the America Online access software — before venturing into the online world. This section is your pre-online checklist of the basics that you need to get into (and out of) America Online — plus some ideas to help your cyberhighway launch.

In this part . . .

- ✔ What You See
- ✔ Toolbar Table
- ✔ The Basics
- ✔ What You Can Do

What You See: The America Online Welcome Window

When you first sign on to America Online, the software presents you with the Welcome window and the AOL screen. This is where your adventure begins. From this window, along with the toolbars and menus that are part of the America Online software, you can visit Web sites, prowl AOL's internal forums or write an electronic mail message. For more information on each of the features identified here, turn to its section.

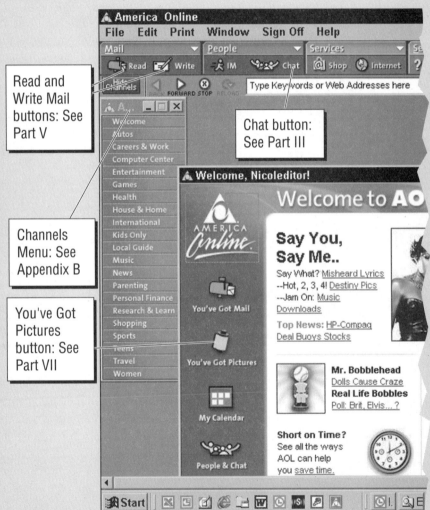

Read and Write Mail buttons: See Part V

Chat button: See Part III

Channels Menu: See Appendix B

You've Got Pictures button: See Part VII

My Favorites button:
See Part II

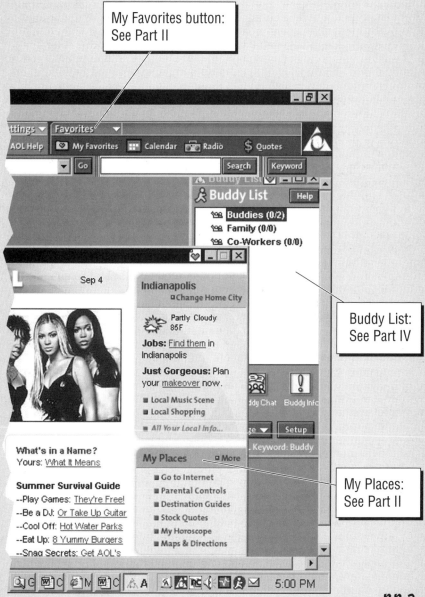

Buddy List:
See Part IV

My Places:
See Part II

What You See: Dialog Boxes

Dialog boxes appear on America Online when the software wants some kind of information from you. To change the folder that contains the files you download from AOL, you use the Download Preferences dialog box. The little Keyword window that you use to launch a keyword on AOL is actually a dialog box. Large and small, these windows help you customize the AOL software, request newsletters, change your dial-up access numbers, and much more.

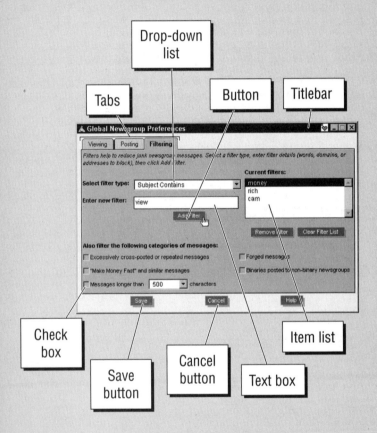

- ✔ **Buttons:** Use buttons to cancel a change, save a change, close a dialog box, select a feature, add or remove a selection, and open the Help system.

- ✔ **Check box:** Select an option by selecting (clicking) the check box in front of it; selecting a marked check box deselects the option. If you like, you can select more than one check box at a time and they will function together.

- ✔ **Drop-down list:** Clicking the down arrow reveals a list of choices. Drag the mouse over the list until you reach the choice you desire. Then click the option that you want to select it.

- ✔ **Item list:** An item list is a group of options that appears in a text box. Click an option to highlight it and then click an action button such as *Remove* or *Add* to alter the list.

- ✔ **Radio buttons (not shown):** Radio buttons work much like check boxes in that you use them to select options. However, with a radio button, you can select only one at a time. Selecting (clicking) one radio button to activate it automatically turns off the others in the group.

- ✔ **Tabs:** Tabs appear near the top of a dialog box to show that the box contains several sections. Click a tab to open that window of information.

- ✔ **Text box:** In text boxes, you enter text, such as a keyword, a folder name, or a search term.

- ✔ **Title bar:** These bars stretch across the top of a dialog box (or any window on America Online, for that matter) and contain the name of the dialog box (or window).

Toolbar Table

The toolbar buttons function in two ways. Buttons *without* a downward-pointing triangle provide a shortcut to either an America Online command (such as Write Mail) or an online area (such as Quotes). Buttons that *do* sport such triangles reveal a pull-down menu when you click them; they function much like menu-bar items.

Tool/Button	Tool Name	What You Can Do	Shortcut	See
Mail	Mail	Look at e-mail you've sent, change e-mail preferences, create a signature file for your e-mail messages, run Automatic AOL, or open your online Address Book.	n/a	Part V
Read	Read	Open a window full of your incoming mail.	Ctrl+R	Part V
Write	Write	Write a new e-mail message.	Ctrl+M	Part V
People	People	Chat, talk, giggle, and laugh in a chat room or locate other members online.	n/a	Part III
IM	IM	Send an Instant Message.	Ctrl+I	Part IV
Chat	Chat	Open the People Connection main window.	n/a	Part III
Services	Services	Visit one of the many featured areas on America Online.	n/a	The Big Picture
Shop	Shop	Give your charge card a workout in one of AOL's many shopping areas.	n/a	Appendix B
Internet	Internet	Hop on the cyberhighway. This button takes you directly to the Internet Connection portion of AOL.com.	n/a	Part IX
Settings	Settings	Change your Preferences, create or delete Screen Names or Passwords, set Parental Controls, or create (or change) your Directory (member profile) Listing.	n/a	Part I

Tool/Button	Tool Name	What You Can Do	Shortcut	See
? AOL Help	AOL Help	Visit the online AOL Help area for America Online assistance.	n/a	Part XI
Favorites ▼	Favorites	Open the Favorite Places window, edit Hot Keys to your favorite AOL areas, or open the Keyword window.	n/a	Part II
My Favorites	My Favorites	Open a window listing your Favorite Places.	n/a	Part II
Calendar	Calendar	Schedule outings, appointments, and other important dates.	n/a	Part I
Radio	Radio	Listen to your favorite tunes through your AOL connection.	n/a	The Big Picture
$ Quotes	Quotes	Track your favorite stocks.	n/a	The Big Picture

The Basics: Signing On

Here's the drill for signing on to America Online:

1. If the America Online software is not already running, start it by double-clicking the America Online icon. The Sign On dialog box appears.

2. If you have more than one screen name, pick the screen name that you want to use this time. Click the down arrow in the Select Screen Name box and then click a screen name.

3. Press Tab to move the cursor into the Enter Password box and then carefully type your password.

    If you're accessing America Online from your home computer, continue to Step 4. If you want to connect to the service from some other location, select that location from the Select Location box. *See also* Part X to create a new location.

4. Take a moment to make sure that your modem is turned on and nobody else in the family is using the phone line. Then press Enter or click the Sign On button. A series of graphics displays your progress toward connecting. America Online may also have a few commercials for you; click Cancel to skip past them. When the Welcome screen appears, you're ready to use America Online.

TIP ✦ If your connection attempt doesn't go through, click Cancel and try again. If the connection still doesn't work, wait a few minutes and then give it one more attempt before you seek help from the support line (1-800-827-3338).

If you repeatedly experience problems connecting to the service, you may try including another local access number. *See also* Part X for all the details.

The Basics: Using Keywords to Open Online Areas

America Online assigns a *keyword* to most of its forums so that you can find them again and again. Keywords are usually easy to guess: the keyword for the Sports channel, for example, is **Sports**. To use a keyword:

1. Press Ctrl+K or click the Keyword button on the browser bar to open the Keyword dialog box.

2. Type the keyword into the text box.

3. Press Enter or click Go.

If you aren't sure about a keyword, give it a try. You might find an area that you never knew existed online.

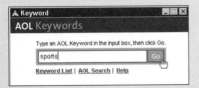

The Basics: Using My Places to Locate Favorite Areas

After browsing America Online for a while, you find yourself returning to the same areas over and over again. Maybe it's the main News window. Or perhaps you set your kitchen clock by the recipes that you download each week. My Places gives you a section right on the main Welcome window that you can use to jump to some of your most-loved AOL areas.

To set My Places:

1. Click the More button in the My Places portion of the Welcome window.

2. Click the Change My Places button in the More window that appears.

3. Select any Choose New Place button to navigate through the drop-down menus that appear. Choose an option from any channel in the list and it appears in red next to the Choose New Places button.

4. When you're finished customizing My Places, click the Save My Changes button. The first six places appear on the Welcome window; clicking the More button reveals the entire list.

The Basics: Getting Online Help

Every now and then, you might stumble upon a problem that requires a little online assistance. If you have a general question about America Online, use keyword **Help** to open the AOL Help main window. AOL Help answers questions about Instant Messages, Buddy Lists, Parental Controls, finding things online, and installing newer versions of the AOL software. To get general computer help, go to the Computer Center Get Help Now window (keyword **Get Help Now**).

See also Part XI for more information on finding help on- and offline.

The Basics: Signing Off America Online

When you finish visiting America Online, always remember to sign off (signing off keeps AOL from having to do it for you).

1. If you started either a chat log or session log, close the log file before leaving America Online. To close the log file, choose File⇨Log Manager and then click the Close Log button.

2. Choose Sign Off⇨Sign Off, and AOL signs you off. The Sign On box reappears, with a friendly Goodbye from America Online! message in the title bar.

3. Choose File⇨Exit or click the Close box in the upper-right corner of the screen to exit the software.

See also "The Basics: Signing On" earlier in this part.

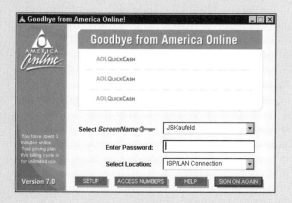

What You Can Do: Read Today's Headlines

America Online excels at bringing the world's news to your computer screen. Whether you want to track the local headlines or read the news halfway across the world, you can use America Online (and its keywords) to keep abreast of happenings everywhere. To read today's headlines, you can

1. Get started by:

Clicking the link next to Top News on the Welcome window, The Big Picture

Using keyword **News** to open the News Channel window, Appendix B

Looking at a state's headlines in the Local Guide Channel, Part II

2. Continue by:

Clicking any of the News Sections buttons in the main News Channel window, Appendix B

Clicking the News Ticker in the main News Channel window, Appendix B

Visiting one of the national news providers, keywords **Time**, **CBS News**, or **NYT**

3. Become a power AOL user by:

Creating a My News profile, Part I

Delving into local newspapers, keyword **Newspapers**

Locating International news, keyword **World News**

What You Can Do: Send an E-Mail Message

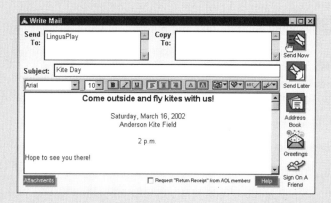

Use America Online to keep up with friends, co-workers, long-lost relatives — basically, anyone with an e-mail account. You simply open an empty Mail window, fill in the address and your message, and send it off. With a little practice, you can even spice up your text with jazzy fonts, attach files or a picture, and drop a standard signature into your messages so everyone will know who you are. To send an e-mail message, you can

1. Get started by:

Opening the Write Mail window, Part V

Sending your message through the Internet, Part V

Locating friends through the Member Directory, Part IV

2. Continue by:

Creating Address Book entries, Part V

Setting your Mail preferences, Part I

Downloading files from e-mail messages, Part VIII

3. Become a power AOL user by:

Formatting your e-mail text, Part V

Creating a signature file, Part V

Sending online photos in e-mail, Part VII

What You Can Do: Research a Topic on the Web

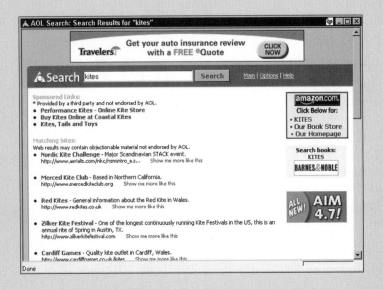

Your America Online connection gives you access to a world of information — in science, current events, computing, hobbies, history, and more. When you want to know about a topic, you can use AOL and the Internet to find out about it. To research a topic on the Web, you can

1. Get started by:

Using AOL Search to look for Web sites, Part IX

Using the AOL Channels to locate information, Part II

Finding an AOL discussion board on your topic, Part VI

2. Continue by:

Marking the best places you find as Favorite Places, Part II

Saving and printing your information, Part VIII

Starting an AOL Group to share your interest, Part VI

3. Become a power AOL user by:

Joining a newsgroup that discusses your topic, Part IX

Creating a Web page that shares what you found, Part IX

Joining a mailing list on your topic, Part IX

Part I

Personalizing Your Corner of the World

Your new America Online account works pretty well right from the start, but with a few tweaks here and there, it becomes a high-performance machine. From account preferences to custom news wires, this part explores the available tools and services that you can use to make America Online uniquely yours.

In this part . . .

Bringing the News to Your Mailbox 2
Changing Your Member Profile 2
Changing Your Password 2
Changing Your Preferences 3
Creating a Screen Name 10
Deleting a Screen Name 12
Limiting Your Child's Online Access 12
Making Your Member Profile 13
My Calendar 14
My News 17
Parental Controls 19
Restoring a Screen Name 22

Bringing the News to Your Mailbox

Sifting through the day's news takes time — after all, a lot of stuff happens every day. AOL helps you save time with a better way to keep up with current events.

With the America Online My News profile system, stories land directly in your e-mailbox, called the Online Mailbox, instead of crowding together in long lists. Best of all, the stories focus on topics that you choose. This setup provides personalized information gathering at its best — and with no extra charge for the service. For details, *see also* the "My News" section later in this part.

Changing Your Member Profile

Some days you feel like yourself; other days, you don't. To tell the world (or at least other America Online members) about these personal variations, change your online profile. In an amazing stroke of simplicity, you use the same steps to both create and change a member profile.

See also "Making Your Member Profile" later in this part; Part IV.

Changing Your Password

Your password is the key to your account. To keep your account safe, change the password every month or so. Pick a password that's hard for other people to guess.

Try making your password from two unrelated words and a number. Combinations such as `coincard3`, `cow8box`, and `clock4pad` may look silly, but they're examples of good passwords.

When you're thinking in the password-vein of things, be sure that you don't use a combination screen name and password that people might easily put together. For instance, if you select *Abbott* as a screen name, using *Costello* as a password might not be wise. In the same vein, the screen name *Bugsy* begs for *Malone* as a matching password. Although this makes your password simple for you to remember, it also becomes incredibly easy for a hacker to guess. Save yourself the grief of a hacked account by skipping the cutesy factor of a matched screen name and password.

To change your password, follow these steps:

1. Use keyword **Password** and then click the *Change password* button.

2. Type your current password into the *Current password* text box, and then press Tab. (The password appears as asterisks on-screen.)

3. Carefully type your new password into the two text boxes at the bottom of the screen. Capitalization doesn't matter, but spelling does. Make sure that your password does not include spaces. The AOL computers don't like spaces too much.

4. When you finish, click the *Change password* button. (If the two new password entries match, AOL changes your password. If they don't match, AOL prompts you to try again.)

After you change your password, be sure to remember it. Forgetting your password comes under the heading of Really Bad Ways to Start Your Day.

See also information on using keywords in Part II.

Changing Your Preferences

The Preferences settings fine-tune your America Online experience. Almost every aspect of online life includes some Preferences settings. Whether you want to save copies of e-mail messages to your Filing Cabinet automatically, turn off the system sound effects, or manage the Personal Filing Cabinet, the Preferences settings cover your needs, offering all the preferences and also throwing in short descriptions of each option at no extra charge.

To change preferences, choose Settings⇨Preferences from the toolbar (or use keyword **Preferences**), and click its link in the list. Each link in the Preferences window takes you right to the dialog box that you need in order to change that America Online option.

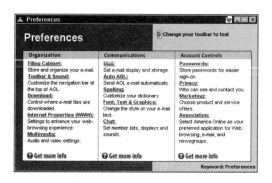

You don't need to sign on to America Online to use the Preferences window — it's always available, so you can save online time and money (especially if you use one of the measured-service pricing plans that AOL offers), by using the Preferences window offline. The offline Preferences window lets you set Communications and Organization controls, but you need to sign onto America Online to alter your Account Controls settings.

Whether you use the Preferences window online or offline, the windows for individual settings are the same.

To learn all the detailed ins and outs regarding America Online preferences, see *America Online 7.0 For Dummies,* by John Kaufeld (Hungry Minds, Inc.).

Here are the current preferences available, along with an idea of what you find when you select an individual preference.

Association

Choosing the Association link in the Preferences window selects America Online as your default application for Internet access. Selecting AOL as your Internet application can save you a lot of frustration if AOL is the only Internet service provider (ISP) that you use. When you click a link in a document and you're not currently online, AOL automatically opens and loads that Web site for you. In comparison, Microsoft Internet Explorer opens, attempts to load a site, and then tells you that it can't reach the Internet (because you don't have an always-on, live Internet connection at your house like most corporations do).

If you use another Internet service or you think you'd ever want to try a separate ISP, do *not* click OK to establish America Online as your default Internet application. When the dialog box tells you that clicking OK sets the change permanently, it means what it says.

Auto AOL

Choosing Auto AOL (short for Automatic AOL) enables you to download new e-mail messages into your computer, send e-mail you've written offline, and get and send any new newsgroup postings that wait for your attention.

You probably want to set your Auto AOL preferences so that you can send mail and get unread mail automatically. I generally leave the *Download files* option unchecked and download each attached file by hand as I need it. That way, I don't mistakenly download and open a hacker's contribution to my hard drive.

Chat

Chat options control the chat room window itself, changing the way that you see all chat rooms on the whole system. The most useful settings here are *Alphabetize the member list* (turn this option on to simplify your life) and *Enable chat room sounds* (turn this option off when someone won't stop playing sounds).

Download

Downloading cool stuff from the file libraries makes life worth living. To make downloading even easier, turn on *Automatically decompress/ expand ZIP files at sign-off.* This choice automatically expands ZIP files after you sign off — it's pretty cool stuff. If you'd rather that AOL decompress the ZIP files immediately after you download the files or leave the files alone so you can decompress them yourself at a later time, the Download window gives you options for that, too.

Two options to turn off are *Delete ZIP files after they are decompressed* and *Confirm when I add files to my download list.* If you want downloads to go to a specific place (other than the default AOL Download folder), this window is where you change the download destination directory.

Filing Cabinet

Although the Personal Filing Cabinet is the neatest thing to hit the online world since high-speed modems, not too many preferences cover it. The only preferences really worth mentioning are the two deletion options: *Confirm before deleting single/multiple items* and *Confirm before deleting multiple items.* If you're confident of your editing skills, turn these options off and save some time. On the other hand, if your life includes small children ("What does the DEL key do, Dad?"), leave these options turned on to protect your carefully filed information.

Font, Text & Graphics

Setting font preferences gives you the flexibility to change the fonts you see in chat rooms, e-mail, and Instant Messages. Be aware, however, that America Online has gone to great lengths to use fonts that are readable. If you choose some esoteric font for your chat rooms, reading the text may become more of a challenge — but hey, that's half the fun!

Also use this window to set the text size for e-mail, chat rooms, and Instant Messages. If you want to fit more words to a window without manually changing the text size each time you send an Instant Message or e-mail, select the *Small text* option. On the other hand, if larger letters would really be of help, select Large as your text-size preference.

One of the most useful items in the Font, Text & Graphics window is the *Maximum disk space to use for online art* setting. If you're low on disk space, try reducing this setting from 40MB to 10MB. (Getting a bigger hard disk would be a *really* good idea, though.)

If you open several windows while you're online, you may come close to the maximum disk space amount you set. When that happens, every window you attempt to open brings a warning dialog box explaining that a graphic on the window can't be displayed because of low memory. Don't panic or run out to purchase a new hard drive — simply return to the Font, Text & Graphics window and increase the *Maximum disk space to use for online art.* Poof! No more annoying dialog boxes.

Internet Properties (WWW)

The Web settings resemble a cross between a 747 cockpit and the control room of your local nuclear power plant. When you tweak the Windows Web preferences, you're actually altering the settings for Microsoft Internet Explorer (IE).

Depending on your level of comfort with complexity, you may want to change several settings in the AOL Internet Properties window. Any alterations here actually change the IE settings, rather than the America Online software itself. Use the tabs at the top of the window to flip among the setting topics:

✓ **General tab:** Look under the General tab to customize link colors and specify the Web page that you want to use as your home page. Here you can also clear the History folder — the list of Web page links you've visited.

If you surf the Web often, you'll want to click Clear History every now and then to empty the folder.

✓ **Security tab:** Use options on the Security tab to set Internet safety preferences. The default setting for general Internet surfing is set at Medium, which prompts you with a warning dialog box when you attempt to download files from Web sites.

The Security tab also allows you to include specific Web sites as Trusted Sites or Restricted Sites by clicking the corresponding icon and then entering the site's Web address in the dialog box that appears. (I recommend that you take the easy way out and set Web preferences in the AOL Parental Controls to shield the kids from harmful content.)

✓ **Content tab:** The Content tab contains a whole collection of things you don't need to mess with as an America Online subscriber. This tab sets Web certificates and other tenets of geekdom. Best to leave these options alone.

✔ **Web Graphics tab:** This tab gives you one lonely option: to compress Web graphics as they load. Leave that one marked to trim a little delay from the World Wide Wait.

Shopping Assistant takes its place as the final tab in the Windows AOL Internet Properties window. Inside you find a check box that offers to show you the America Online Shopping Assistant each time that you shop online. Selecting this check box doesn't seem to do a whole lot; check or uncheck it, as you prefer.

Mail

The most useful e-mail preferences you can change are *Close mail after it has been sent* and *Use my address book to auto-suggest e-mail addresses*. America Online checks both these options for you by default. Without setting the Close mail option, your e-mail message sits and looks at you after you send it. If you click the Send button again (just to make sure your message is sent), your e-mail recipient receives multiple copies of your message. Better to check the box and save yourself some headaches.

The Auto-suggest option automatically finishes entering the e-mail address of your mail recipient if you've added that person's e-mail address to your Address Book. You begin by typing the first letter or two, and AOL helpfully suggests a list of e-mail addresses (taken from your Address Book) that match those letters. Unless all the names in your Address Book begin with the same two or three letters, this option saves you a lot of time if you write a lot of e-mail messages.

On a related note, I recommend turning off the *Confirm that mail has been sent* option. If you send more than two e-mail messages each month, this option gets *very* old *very* fast.

Nestled at the bottom of the Reading Mail options, check out the option *Keep my old mail online X days after I read it*. This default is set to three days; I recommend setting it to seven days, which is as high as the setting goes, and here's why: AOL zaps read e-mail messages by the *send* date rather than the *first-read* date — if you read a message that arrived in your box four days ago and you want to reread it from your Read Mail list the next morning, that message will be history unless you increase the number of days that AOL keeps your old mail.

Marketing

Call me a hermit-in-the-making, but I'm burned out on junk mail and "Have we got an offer for you" phone calls. If you're like me, then run — don't walk — to the Marketing Preferences window. Here is your chance to strike a blow for empty mailboxes and quiet phone lines.

The Marketing Preferences dialog box is available through keyword **Marketing Prefs**. (It's also in the Preferences window, but why bother?)

1. In the Marketing Preferences dialog box, click the button next to your pet peeve. Your choices are U.S. Mail From Other Organizations, U.S. Mail From AOL, Telephone, E-mail, Pop-up, and Additional Information.

(*Pop-up* is America Online's term for those advertising dialog boxes that appear occasionally when you sign onto the system. When you select a topic, a brief dialog box appears that explains why this particular type of junk mail is desirable.)

2. Click the Continue button, and then choose either *Yes I do want . . .* or *No I don't.*

3. Then click OK to make it so.

Two other options deserve a quick mention as tools of a dedicated anti-annoyance crusader. Take a look at the Direct Marketing Association Mail Preference Service and Telephone Preference Service choices for details on how to *truly* remove yourself (at least temporarily) from the world of junk communications. You'll find addresses for both these organizations under the Additional Information button.

Multimedia

The Multimedia Preferences window contains two settings, Player Preferences and Accessibility Preferences.

Choose Player Preferences to use the AOL Media Player for supported file types. Keep this one checked unless you've collected other players during your Internet excursions and you prefer to use one or more of those. The other Player Preferences option is *Use the AOL Media Player as my default CD player.* This one is entirely your call. I prefer the internal CD player that came with my computer; if you like yours, stick with it. If you want to give the AOL Media Player a try, check the box. You can always uncheck it later.

Choose the second Multimedia setting, Accessibility Preferences, to show captions along with multimedia when they're available. One example of captions in action is printed words along with news slide shows. Check *Display captions when available* to see for yourself.

Passwords

If you're tired of typing your screen name and password every time you sign on to America Online, use this preference setting to fix the problem once and for all. Type the password next to its associated screen name, and America Online won't ever ask you about it again.

Unfortunately, anyone who wanders by can then sign on to your account without knowing the password, so use this option only if your computer is in a secure area.

Privacy

Decide who you want to be able to contact you and make your preferences known in the Privacy Preferences window. By default, the preference is set to *Allow all AOL members and AOL Instant Message users to see you on their buddy lists and send you Instant Messages.* If you want to exclude a few select people or you want to welcome only a designated group of screen names into your online world, you can do that, too. (You can also get to this window by clicking the Privacy Preferences button in your Buddy List Setup window. Open the window with keyword **Buddy**.)

Spelling

The Spelling preference enables you to set your America Online software to capitalize the first word in a sentence, notify you if you type the same word twice, and choose a preferred dictionary (instead of the default AOL U.S. English dictionary) for spell-checking. All Spelling preferences are turned on; if you really know your grammar and want a challenge, turn any of them off. Otherwise, leave them on — you now have one less thing to worry about.

Toolbar & Sound

Play around with the toolbar at the top of the screen. Would you prefer icons along the top of the screen, or simply text buttons? Toolbar preferences allow you to change how the toolbar looks and where it appears (at the top or bottom of your screen). One of its most useful features is that you can set the preferences to clear your History Trail each time that you sign off. Doing so deletes that long list of windows you opened while online — which the America Online software diligently keeps track of, just in case you want to return to a window you saw yesterday (or even last week).

Check *Clear History after each Sign-off* or *Switch Screen Name* if you want the AOL software to clean the slate each time that you leave. To delete the list yourself, click the Clear History Now button, and then click Yes when you're queried about whether you really want to erase your trail.

This window also allows you to turn off AOL sounds such as You've Got Mail and the Buddy List sounds. Uncheck *Enable AOL sounds* (such as the Welcome greeting and Instant Message chimes) if you want a quiet America Online experience. On the other hand, it might be easier to just reach up and turn off your speakers.

Creating a Screen Name

Part of the fun on America Online is creating cool screen names that contribute to your online identity. Many people use more than one screen name, often using one for work and another for play. If your kids are online and you want to use the Parental Controls to limit their activities, then the kids need individual screen names, too. Each account has space for a primary screen name (the name you create when you sign up for America Online) and up to six secondary names.

America Online allows you to create more than one master screen name for an account, in case you have more than one adult in a household (or at least, more than one person over 18 years old). Your primary screen name automatically classifies as a master screen name. All master screen names have the capability to change America Online billing options and set Parental Controls for all the other screen names on the master screen names' account. If you already have seven screen names in the account, you can't make a new one until you delete an old one. Sorry, but that's just how these things go.

To create a screen name, follow these steps:

1. Before signing on to America Online, think up a few possible screen names and write them down. (That way, if someone else snarfed up the name you wanted, you won't waste online time trying to think up another, equally cool name to replace it.)

2. Sign on using the master screen name. Only a user bearing the master screen name can create new screen names.

3. Use keyword **Screen Names**. The Screen Names dialog box appears.

4. Click *Create a screen name.* AOL first asks you whether you're creating this screen name for a child. If you click Yes, AOL then presents you with a window explaining the Parental Controls feature. Click the Continue button to move on.

   The Create a Screen Name dialog box appears, which explains that the screen name you create will be public.

5. Click the Create Screen Name button to continue. The Choose a Screen Name dialog box appears.

6. Carefully type the screen name you want into the box at the bottom of the screen. Double-check the spelling, and then click the Continue button.

   If the name is available, congratulations! The Choose a Password dialog box pops up to announce your success.

On the other hand, if someone else already has that screen name, AOL informs you that the specific name is already in use. Whip out that list of backup names and keep trying until something works.

At this point, AOL offers to create a screen name for you. The Choose Another Screen Name dialog box appears, with the Suggest a Screen Name option checked and ready to go. If you want some help from the system that already knows which names are taken, you can enter words into the three text boxes and AOL suggests a screen name option for you. Or you can click the button next to Try another Screen Name and continue on your own. (Your best bet might be to try names on your own. The AOL screen name generator isn't very bright, and it comes up with some pretty silly alternatives.)

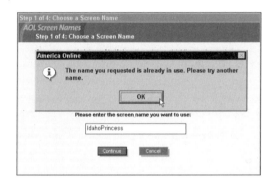

7. Type a password for the new screen name; then press Tab and type it again. When you finish, click the Continue button. If you type the same password in both boxes, AOL congratulates you by presenting yet another dialog box. If you mistyped one of the passwords, AOL asks you to try doing the password thing one more time.

8. A Parental Controls dialog box jumps to the screen. Select the age range of the screen name's owner, and America Online automatically installs its Parental Controls on that screen name. Click the Continue button.

If you select 18+ as the age range for the new screen name, AOL asks whether you want the new screen name to function as a Master Screen name, complete with the power to change billing options and set Parental Controls for all other screen names on the account. If you don't want the new screen name holder to exercise that much freedom, select No.

9. A final Confirm Your Settings dialog box appears, listing your new screen name and the access features that go along with the age range you selected. If everything looks okay to you, press Enter (or click Accept Settings) to accept the settings and create your new screen name.

America Online then creates the screen name and adds it to your access software. It appears in the AOL Screen Names window, taking its place as the last created name in the Your current Screen Names list. Congratulations — you're now the owner of a new, unique AOL screen name.

See also "Parental Controls" later in this part.

Deleting a Screen Name

When the time comes to bid a fond farewell to a screen name, don't get too sentimental — just delete the little fellow. You can delete any of the six secondary screen names on your account. However, you can't delete the primary screen name (you're stuck with that one forever).

1. Sign on to AOL with the master screen name. Only a user bearing the master screen name can delete another screen name.

2. Use keyword **Screen Names**. (The Screen Names dialog box hops into action.)

3. Click the *Delete a screen name* button; then click Continue in the *Are you really sure you want to do this?* dialog box. The Delete dialog box morosely takes the stage, displaying only your account's secondary screen names. (**Remember:** You can't delete the primary screen name.)

4. Click the screen name that you want to delete; then click Delete. After a moment, a dialog box pops up and announces the screen name's demise.

 If you make a horrible mistake and accidentally delete your favorite gaming or hobby screen name, AOL has a Restore a Screen Name feature. **See also** "Restoring a Screen Name" later in this part.

Limiting Your Child's Online Access

America Online resembles a large metropolitan city. AOL offers libraries full of information, open spaces to meet and play, and a business district humming with life. Unfortunately, the metaphor goes further — America Online also harbors some less-than-desirable neighborhoods.

Just as you wouldn't send a child into the bad parts of the city (or into the mall alone with your charge card), you don't necessarily want little eyes and fingers to command full access to America Online and the Internet. That's where the Parental Controls come in. The Parental Controls are your tools for steering and blocking an impressionable child's access to online content.

To find out the specifics, *see also* "Parental Controls" later in this part.

Making Your Member Profile

Your Member Profile tells the world who you are, what you think, and why you exist on the planet. If you want everyone on America Online to know something about you, put the information into your profile. If you want to remain an online enigma (and I know lots of AOL members who do) you don't have to create a profile at all.

To create a profile:

1. Use keyword **Profile** to open the Member Directory window.

2. Click the My Profile button. The Edit Your Online Profile window appears, but the window is unreadable because of the large warning dialog box that jumps to the screen directly on top of the Profile window. The warning dialog box begins by telling you that your AOL Member Profile is available to be seen by all America Online members. Then it suggests that no member include personal information in *any* profile — all good stuff to know.

3. Click OK after you read through the helpful dialog box and proceed with your regularly scheduled member profile. If you never want to see the warning again, check *Please do not show me this again* and then click OK.

4. Enter your information into the spaces in the profile window. Include as little or as much information as you like; some members include only their screen names and general geographic location, and others complete each line and even include a personal quote.

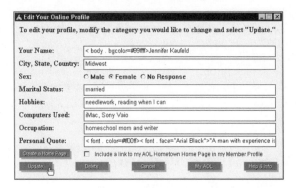

5. **Click the Update button to store your changes; click the Cancel button to forget the changes.** Within a few minutes (sometimes longer), the new profile proudly takes its place in the Member Directory.

If you want to include more information than the profile allows, try creating your own Web page. Clicking the Create a Home Page button in the Edit Your Online Profile window takes you to AOL Hometown, where you can upload your current Web page (if you have one) or design a new one. You can also get there with keyword **Hometown**.

America Online gives you the capability to customize your profile. John Kaufeld's *America Online 7.0 For Dummies,* (Hungry Minds, Inc.) contains a whole chapter on cool profile tricks.

See also Parts III and IV for more on using profiles.

My Calendar

If you find yourself scheduling appointments or events with friends and colleagues via e-mail; if you want to know about that movie, IPO, or audio CD *before* it's released; or if you need an all-in-one organizer to plan family outings, business occasions, and never-ending trips to the vet; then you'll love My Calendar. My Calendar helps you to fill your days as full as you like.

With My Calendar, you can:

 ✔ See a pictorial five-day weather forecast each time that you open My Calendar. If you plan a lot of outdoor activities, this feature is quite handy.

 ✔ Color-code your appointments. Choose a different color for each person in the family, or select colors by category so that you know the type of activity at a glance.

- ✔ Get detailed information on any appointment by clicking its entry.

- ✔ Switch between daily, weekly, and monthly calendar screens with the click of a tab.

- ✔ Edit any appointment by clicking the entry and then changing the information in the dialog box that appears.

To customize My Calendar:

1. Use keyword **Calendar** to open My Calendar in the browser window, or click the My Calendar button in the Welcome window. My Calendar blazes to life.

2. To add an appointment of your own to the calendar, click the Add button.

3. In the Appointment Details screen that appears, type in a title for your appointment, and then select its date, time, and duration from the drop-down lists.

   Select the type of entry from the Type drop-down list. Choices include everything from Birthday and Meeting to Travel or Wedding. If you want, you can even color-code your entry so that it stands out.

   If the event takes place at no particular time of day, such as an anniversary or vacation day, leave the Untimed selection visible.

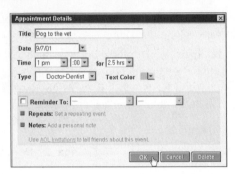

4. If your appointment recurs on a daily, weekly, or monthly basis, click the Repeats link and enter the details in the resulting window.

5. Click the Notes link in the Appointment Details window to enter any reminders or details that you need to remember, such as a *Bring earplugs* reminder for drum lessons.

6. When you're finished, click OK to include this entry in your calendar.

Use the tabs at the top of the page to view your calendar entries by the month, week, or day.

One of the coolest My Calendar features is that you can include current and upcoming events from many different areas of your life. To see the range of available appointments and events, click the Event Directory Go button. Best of all, the calendar links with the Local Guide channel so that you can even include upcoming local events in your online calendar. Some favorite Event Directory items include:

✔ **Concerts and CDs:** Mark your calendar with upcoming concerts in your area and CD releases so that you don't miss ticket sales or overlook that CD you've wanted.

✔ **Holidays:** Select from holidays from around the world as well as various religious traditions. Want to ensure that you don't miss Bastille Day next year? Put it on your calendar.

✔ **Festivals:** Pack up the car and take the family to your favorite festival. Include events from your hometown, your favorite city, or an area that you want to visit someday.

✔ **Earnings, IPOs, and Splits:** Let My Calendar remind you of those upcoming Initial Public Offerings and stock splits, and you can give your stockbroker's phone line a rest.

✔ **Pro and College Teams:** Put your favorite team's schedule on the calendar and you'll know when to make the popcorn.

If you want to print your calendar, click the printer icon next to the More button in your calendar's window. To print a daily list of events, click the Day tab and then click the printer icon.

Add a new appointment without opening the My Calendar window. Keyword **Add2Cal** opens a small Add to My Calendar appointment window. Give your appointment a title, select a date and time, and click Add to My Calendar.

My News

Studying current events in China? Keeping an eye on your company's competition? Looking for the latest tidbits about your favorite team? Stop searching for stories the hard way — let the news come to you with a My News profile.

My News profiles are personalized news services that constantly scan for stories that contain terms you specify. Each profile captures up to 50 stories per day from news sources, such as Reuters World Service, PR Newswire, Business Wire, Sports Ticker, *Variety*, and others. Whatever your news needs, the America Online My News profile system delivers the latest stories straight to your e-mail box. Best of all, using My News involves no extra fee.

To enroll in My News, follow these steps:

1. Get into the My News area with keyword **My News**. (The My News browser window appears.)

2. To set up your first profile, click the Go to Step 1 button. To make another profile, click the <u>Create a New Profile</u> link. The Select Your Categories screen opens with an amazing number of checkable options.

   Check the topics that you want to include in your profile. Because you can have several profiles searching the Web at once, you may want to keep each profile to a narrow subject or topic set. Including mining and metals, music, and media in one profile can get pretty confusing unless you want to call it *Profile M.*

   To change or delete a profile, click the Modify or Delete button next to the profile's name. You can also turn your profile off at will without deleting it if your e-mail box overflows or you want to take a break from the news.

3. Click the Next Step button when you finish selecting the category (or categories) for your profile. The Add Search Terms window opens.

4. Enter any words that you want to help define your search. If you want to narrow a textile search to deliver only stories about the Singer Company, for example, type **Singer** into the Required Terms text box. If you want all information about textiles except the Singer Company, then type **Singer** into the *Do NOT deliver articles...present* text box. (This is especially helpful if you want to engage in a little competitive research, and you work for the company in question. You already know what's going on there, so you have no need to read news releases and articles that highlight your own firm.)

5. Click the Next Step button when you're ready to continue. The Confirm Your Choices window appears. If you want to change any of the categories or search terms you created earlier, you can do that now.

6. Give your profile a name by typing it into the *Name your profile* text box. Then select the number of articles you want to see in your e-mail box each day by choosing a number from the drop-down item list next to *Choose the number of articles a day*. The default setting is 5, and the selection box allows up to 200 messages per day. Unless you want to live at your AOL e-mail window, you probably want to keep the influx to anywhere between 5 and 15 messages per day.

7. Click the Preview Profile button. The window that appears gives you a sample of articles from your new profile. If you like what you see, click the Finish button. If you want more or less results, click the Modify button to alter your profile setup.

That's all there is to it! You just created a My News profile to deliver your kind of news right to your e-mail box.

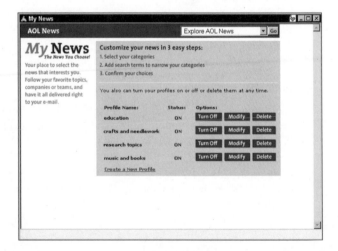

Parental Controls

Keeping kids safe today is tougher than ever before, particularly when the kids have online access. That's why America Online created the Parental Controls. These tools help parents place simple, enforceable boundaries in the freewheeling cyberworld.

With Parental Controls, members either set global controls that cover a child's entire account based on that child's age and maturity level, or they pick and choose from a set of specific custom controls to tailor the Parental Controls to each individual child. The choice is yours.

The General Parental Controls apply sweeping, broad controls to individual screen names based on the child's age. Quick to set, these options give you a good amount of filtering with little software tweaking.

Three levels of control are available:

✔ **Kids Only:** This one-size-fits-all blanket restriction limits your child's screen name to content in the Kids Only channel within America Online, as well as to Kids Only-approved Internet sites. Child Access accounts have no access to America Online's Premium Services — those options that carry an extra price tag, such as AOLbyPhone and some online games. For kids under 12, this level is your best option.

✔ **Young Teen:** Older children (those in the 13–15 age group) need a bit more flexibility to explore the online environment. Young Teen access balances a child's longing for unrestrained command of the world with a parent's goal of not letting the child out of the front yard. AOL's Young Teen controls govern chat areas, download libraries, games, certain Web sites, and the Internet newsgroups. Use these tools to gradually broaden your child's online horizons while shielding your child from the truly heinous stuff. (Properly set, the Teen Access option also functions as the wired equivalent of a grounding.)

✔ **Mature Teen:** This setting, designed for mature teens aged 16–18, allows almost everything on the system. Certain "mature content" Web sites are blocked from these accounts, and the setting also blocks access to premium services (those games and extra AOL add-ons that carry a service charge).

Setting Up a General Parental Controls

Before applying Parental Controls, create a screen name for your child. The child should use her own screen name for online access.

1. Sign on to America Online by using your master screen name. (Only someone using the master screen name has access to the Parental Controls.)

2. Use keyword **Parental Controls** or choose Settings⇨Parental Controls from the toolbar. Either way, the Parental Controls window appears.

3. Click the Set Parental Controls button. The Parental Controls window hops to the screen.

4. Use the drop-down menu to select the screen name that's destined for the new controls.

5. To enable age-specific controls, click Kids Only, Young Teen, or Mature Teen, depending on the child's age and maturity. When you change the screen's age-group category, a dialog box appears explaining the changes you're about to implement.

6. Click the Accept New Category button.

7. Click OK to close the *Your changes to Category Settings have been saved* dialog box.

To remove the age-specific controls, follow the same steps and click the General Access button in Step 5.

To paraphrase the classic warning labels, Parental Controls are not substitutes for parental supervision. I'm not saying that you should hover over your children while they're online. Rather, understand how they use America Online and look for ways to share the experience with them. The best way to ensure that your child remains safe on the Internet is to sit with them and explore the Web together as a special time with parent and child.

Use the Custom Controls button in the Parental Controls window to set controls on e-mail so that the kids can't send or receive pictures or files. This button also lets you limit Instant Messages for the child's screen name.

See also "Creating a Screen Name" earlier in this part, and "Setting Up Custom Controls," next in this part.

Setting Up Custom Controls

Custom Controls enable you to set specific parameters for online access. If you want to increase (or restrict) any child's access in one or more specific areas, use Custom Controls to set access to chats, downloading, newsgroups, e-mail, premium games, or the Web.

1. From the Parental Controls window, click the Set Parental Controls button. The Parental Controls window appears on screen.

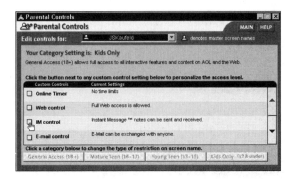

2. Select the child's screen name from the drop-down list.

3. Click the button for the custom control (Online Timer, Web Control, IM Control, E-mail control, Chat control, Additional Master, Download Control, Newsgroup, and Premium Services) that you want to set.

The controls that I recommend selecting are marked with an asterisk (*).

- **E-Mail Control:** *Allow all e-mail to be delivered to this Screen Name*; *Block all e-mail from being delivered to this Screen Name*; *Customize Main Controls for this Screen Name**.

  After you click the *Customize Mail Controls for this Screen Name* button, click Next or click the People and Places tab to see five option buttons with various combinations of e-mail sources that you either block or allow. Read through these options carefully and select the one that best suits the child you're setting controls for.

Click the Pictures and files tab and select one of these options: *Allow this screen name to send and receive mail with pictures and files*; *Block this screen name from sending and receiving mail with pictures and files**.

- **Chat Control:** *Block All AOL Chat*; *Block People Connection featured rooms*; *Block member-created rooms**; *Block all non-People Connection rooms*; *Block viewing and using hyperlinks in rooms**.

- **IM Control:** *Block Instant Message notes**.

  Blocking Instant Messages is a two-edged sword. On one hand, it ensures that your children won't be bothered by strangers; on the other hand, if they want to use America Online's homework help system, their Instant Messages need to be unblocked so that the volunteer teachers can work with them. It's your call.

- **Web Control:** Kids Only (12 and Under); Young Teens (13 to 15); Mature Teens (16 to 17); General Access (18 and older).

- **Additional Master:** Designate this screen name as a master screen name.

- **Download Control:** *Block AOL Software Library Downloads*; *Block FTP Downloads**.

- **Newsgroup:** *Block all newsgroups*; *Block Expert Add of Newsgroups**; *Block Newsgroup File Download**; *Block Adult-Content Newsgroups**; *Block Newsgroups whose titles Contain These Words** (enter the words **sex** and **erotic** — that covers the most colorful newsgroups); *Block the following newsgroups.*

- **Premium Services:** Block Premium Services*.

4. Click Save to save your changes.

   You're rewarded with the *Your changes have been saved* dialog box that congratulates you on work well done.

5. Click OK to make that dialog box go away.

Restoring a Screen Name

Not so long ago, if you deleted a favorite screen name by mistake, and decided that you wanted it back, you were out of luck. However, America Online now provides a way to reactivate those hasty (or erroneous) screen name deletions.

1. Sign on to AOL with the master screen name.

2. Use keyword **Screen Names** to open the AOL Screen Names window.

3. Click the Restore a Screen Name button. If you recently deleted one or more screen names from your account, the Recover Previous Screen Name window hops onto the screen, helpfully listing the deleted screen names.

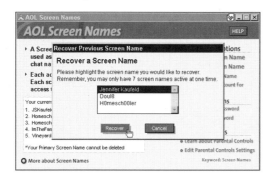

4. Highlight the screen name that you want to rescue and click the Recover button.

5. The system reinstates your screen name and updates your screen name list.

Part II

Navigating Here, There, and Everywhere

Wonderful gems abound on America Online, but you have to know how to find them. This part shows you how to locate areas and services on America Online and tells you what to do with a treasure when you find one.

In this part . . .

Adding Something to Your Favorite Places List . . . 26

Browsing the Channels 26

Building Your Own HotKeys List 27

Changing Something in the Favorite Places List . . 28

Deleting Items from the Favorite Places List 29

Favorite Places 30

Finding Almost Anything on America Online 30

Flipping between Windows 31

Getting a List of Keywords 31

Going to a Favorite Place 32

Locating Keywords 33

Organizing Favorite Places 33

Remembering Your Favorite Online Spots 34

Selecting My Places 34

Using a Keyword 36

Adding Something to Your Favorite Places List

When something is so neat that you want to remember where you saw it, add it to your Favorite Places list. To use the Favorite Places feature, follow these steps:

1. While looking at an online area or Web site, fall deeply in love with it. Convince yourself that you must be able to return there at any time.

2. In the upper right-hand corner of the window icon, you see an icon that looks like a heart on a white sheet of paper with the edge turned down. That's the Favorite Places icon. Click it.

   A small American Online dialog box appears, asking whether you want to save this site in your Favorite Places, insert it into an Instant Message, insert it into an e-mail message, or add it to your Toolbar.

3. Click the Add to Favorites button. The online area's address and name are now part of your Favorite Places list.

See also "Favorite Places," "Going to a Favorite Place," and "Organizing Favorite Places" later in this part.

Browsing the Channels

Opening automatically on the screen each time you sign on to America Online, the Channels list is your doorway to the online world. Channels cover everything in the service from sports to shopping. Click a channel's button and explore. You'll find the channel buttons arranged, in alphabetical order, down the left side of your screen.

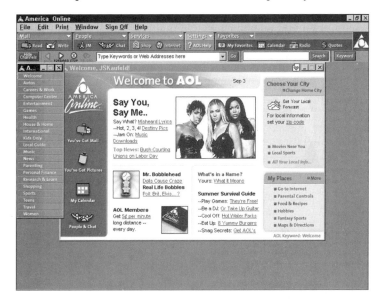

For more information on each channel's contents, check out *America Online 7.0 For Dummies,* by John Kaufeld (Hungry Minds, Inc.).

Building Your Own HotKeys List

If you visit a specific area on AOL so often that you feel like you live there, create a shortcut to the place by including it in your personal HotKeys list. These items use preset keystroke commands, Ctrl+1 through Ctrl+0. To customize your Shortcut Key list:

1. Choose Favorites⇨My Hot Keys.

2. Select Edit My HotKeys from the drop-down menu. The Edit My HotKeys window opens.

3. Replace the existing Menu Entries with favorites of your own. Enter the area's keyword in the text box appearing next to the area's name.

4. Click the Save Changes button.

Shortcut Title	Keyword/Internet Address	Key
Hobbies	hobbies	Ctrl + 1
Start-Up Businesses	startup	Ctrl + 2
Calendar	Calendar	Ctrl + 3
Help	Help	Ctrl + 4
Pets	pets	Ctrl + 5
Get Help Now	get help now	Ctrl + 6
News	News	Ctrl + 7
Shopping	shopping	Ctrl + 8
AOL Live	aol live	Ctrl + 9
What's New	What's New	Ctrl + 0

Edit My Hot Keys — Save Changes / Cancel / Help

If your shortcut key doesn't work, check the keyword's spelling. That's the most likely problem.

See also "Remembering Your Favorite Online Spots" later in this part.

Changing Something in the Favorite Places List

Change is part of the online world's nature. Web page addresses change from time to time, forums reorganize, or maybe you just thought of a better name for that folder that holds the miscellaneous best of the best. Update your Favorite Places list by modifying it:

1. Choose Favorites⇨Favorite Places.

2. Highlight the item you want to change.

3. Click the Edit button.

If you highlighted a Favorite Place entry, a dialog box appears that contains two text boxes. Alter the place name, the address, or both.

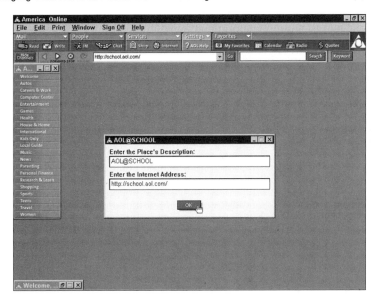

TIP

When you highlight a folder, a cursor appears at the end of the highlighted folder name. Use the Backspace key to erase the part of the folder's name you want to change.

4. Make the changes to your Favorite Place and then click OK. On a folder, change the name and then click the folder icon or anywhere in the Favorite Places window to set your changes.

See also "Favorite Places" later in this part.

Deleting Items from the Favorite Places List

New things lose their charm. When a Favorite Place's luster fades, delete it. Follow these steps:

1. Choose Favorites⇨Favorite Places.

2. Highlight the Favorite Place in question.

3. Click the Delete button at the bottom of the window.

   A dialog box asks whether you're sure you want to delete the item.

4. Click the Yes button to reassure AOL that you do want to kiss your Favorite Place good-bye.

If you're concerned that the item disappears without AOL asking your permission, you need to set your Filing Cabinet Preferences to confirm with you before it deletes single items.

See also "Favorite Places" next in this part.

Favorite Places

Favorite Places is the bookmark feature of America Online. Use it to remember an area, window, or chat room too good to forget. Put forums, Web pages, chat rooms, or message boards into the Favorite Places list. Any window that contains a Favorite Places icon (that white, dog-eared page with the red heart) in the upper right-hand corner qualifies as a potential Favorite Place.

When you discover a wonderful discussion board buried three or four levels deep in the America Online message-board hierarchy, drop that discussion board into your Favorite Places list so that you can find it later and see who responded to your comments. You can even drop news articles and e-mail messages into your Favorite Places list. As long as the window sports a Favorite Places icon, it's fair game.

Your software comes with several Favorite Places already installed. Open the Favorite Places window and then double-click on any folder to open it, revealing Favorite Places to explore.

See also "Adding Something to Your Favorite Places List," "Changing Something in the Favorite Places List," "Deleting Items from the Favorite Places List," "Going to a Favorite Place," "Organizing Favorite Places," and "Remembering Your Favorite Online Spots," all in this part.

Finding Almost Anything on America Online

Use the AOL Search feature to locate nearly everything on America Online — channels, window contents, Web links, the Member Directory, and more. Use the Search button on the Welcome screen to take you to the Search feature.

Open the general AOL Search window and begin a search in a jiffy by typing your topic into the text box on the browser bar and then clicking the Search button. The AOL Search engine returns a list of Web sites that meet your search criteria and suggests related searches among news articles, the Member Directory, international phone books, pictures, and more.

Flipping between Windows

Sooner or later, the windows pile up onscreen. Somewhere at the bottom lies the window you seek. To locate the lost window, either look in the Window menu or press Ctrl+Tab.

✔ Choose Window⌐⊃# (where # is 1 through 9) to go directly to a window. If more than nine windows are open and none is the window you want, choose Window⌐⊃More Windows.

✔ Press Ctrl+Tab to cycle through the windows one at a time. Each press of the key combination reveals another window.

Getting a List of Keywords

Think of keywords as shortcuts through a city. Instead of navigating menus and windows, you type a word or short phrase, and the window opens. Best of all, getting a current list of all America Online keywords is easy.

1. Press Ctrl+K or click the Keyword button on the browser bar to open the Keyword window.

2. Type **Keyword** into the text field.

3. Click the Go button. The Keyword: Keyword window appears.

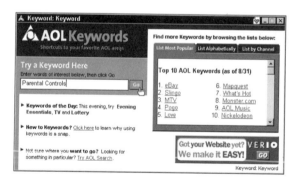

4. Click the List by Channel tab at the top of the list box, on the right side of the window. Finding a specific keyword is much easier when you begin with a general topic than trying to filter through the alphabetical-by-keyword list.

5. Choose a channel to explore and double-click it to see a list of that channel's available keywords.

When America Online redesigned the keyword area, the ability to download the keyword list was removed. To get a copy for your hard drive, open each channel's list individually, highlight the text, and copy it to a new text file (using File⇔New). Then save the text file(s) under some appropriate name. Unless you're one of those "memorize the keywords in A-B-C order" people, you'll survive quite nicely by accessing the keyword list online. Downloading the entire list takes some work; the keyword list is huge.

Although browsing the alphabetical lists takes a bit more time, you can always use the List Alphabetically tab to unearth a keyword gem or two. After you find an area that you like, click the Favorite Places tab to mark that window as a favorite. Otherwise, you either need to memorize the keyword or rifle through the keyword lists to find it again.

Keywords change all the time as new keywords appear and non-functioning ones phase out. Be prepared for AOL to tell you that it can't find some of the keywords.

See also "Locating Keywords" and "Using a Keyword" later in this part.

Going to a Favorite Place

After you find a really cool area, place it among your Favorite Places. You return to that area by following these steps:

1. Choose Favorites⇔Favorite Places. The Favorite Places window opens.

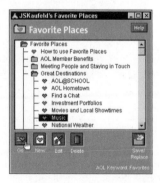

2. Double-click the place's heart icon from your Favorite Places list or highlight the place and click the Go button at the bottom of the window.

In AOL 7.0, your Favorite Places fall into line at the bottom of the Favorites pull-down menu. For a quick trip to one of your favorite areas, follow these simple steps:

1. Click the Favorites toolbar button.

2. Click your chosen Favorite Place to open its window.

Any folders you create appear in the Favorites menu, too. Rest your cursor over the folder, and its contents pop up in a secondary menu for easy selection.

Another way to reveal your Favorite Places window fast is to click the My Favorites button on the Toolbar. Quick and easy.

See also "Favorite Places" earlier in this part.

Locating Keywords

Most main menu screens and many individual forums sport their own keywords. Look for keywords in the lower right-hand corner of the window or on the window's top blue bar. (Sometimes the information hides in another corner, but the lower right-hand location is standard.) The text is small and reads Keyword: (or KW:) with the specific keyword after the colon.

Organizing Favorite Places

After months of surfing the Net, hanging out in online areas, and meeting new friends in various chat rooms, your Favorite Places list might look more like a holiday shopping list or estate auction catalog than an organized selection of special online spots. Before you experience the frustration of scrolling up and down the Favorite Places window looking for a link that escapes you, take a few moments and drop like-minded Favorite Places into folders. Your sanity — and your Favorite Places window — will thank you.

If the Favorite Places list becomes overwhelming, organize it by creating folders that contain categories of places:

1. Choose Favorites⇨Favorite Places.

2. Click the New button at the bottom of the Favorite Places window.

3. Click the New Folder radio button and enter a folder name into the text field.

4. Click OK. The folder appears at the bottom of the Favorite Places list.

5. Click and drag Favorite Places entries to the folder, dropping them in.

Use the same technique to move the folder itself. Just click and drag it to a new location. (You can even put folders inside other folders!)

See also "Adding Something to Your Favorite Places List," "Changing Something in the Favorite Places List," "Deleting Items from the Favorite Places List," "Favorite Places," "Going to a Favorite Place," and "Remembering Your Favorite Online Spots," all in this part.

Remembering Your Favorite Online Spots

Returning to neat places becomes half the fun when you cruise the system. To remember your favorite online spots:

✔ Use the Favorite Places feature.

✔ Set up the My Places feature.

✔ Customize your Hot Keys list.

If you spend a great deal of time online, you may want to customize the Hot Keys list to include the places you visit each time you sign on to America Online, and reserve Favorite Places for really cool places elsewhere online or on the Web.

For more information about cool Favorite Places tricks, as well as customizing your toolbar with the best and brightest places of your heart, see John Kaufeld's *America Online 7.0 For Dummies* (Hungry Minds, Inc.).

See also "Building Your Own HotKeys List" and "Favorite Places" in this part.

Selecting My Places

Think of AOL's My Places feature as a controlled Favorite Places list. Although you can't select from every keyword on the service, My Places enables you to select from many of the most popular online areas.

After you set up your individualized list, you can click one of the buttons in the My Places list to go directly to that area. Look for My Places in the Welcome window.

You can select up to ten favorite online destinations for My Places. Your top six selections appear on the Welcome window under the My Places title, and the others hide behind the More button. To set up My Places, click More and follow these steps:

1. Click the Change My Places button to open the Change My Places screen.

2. Click the first Choose New Place button and highlight a channel from the list that appears.

3. Click to select an area from the channel you highlight. The new place you chose shows up in red, and that area takes its place in the first My Places slot.

4. Continue until you fill all the slots.

5. Click the Save My Changes button to save your changes.

6. A dialog box appears to tell you that AOL saved your selections. Click OK to make the box go away.

You can select each of your favorite areas from different channels or choose them from the same channel if you like.

To change your selections, click More in the My Places portion of the Welcome window, click Change My Places, and choose new areas.

Using a Keyword

Many areas on America Online use their own keywords. To use a keyword, follow these steps:

1. Press Ctrl+K and choose Favorites⇨Go To Keyword from the toolbar, or click the Keyword button on the browser bar. The Keyword dialog box hops into action.

2. Type the keyword into the text field.

3. Click the Go button (or press Enter).

With AOL 7.0, you have yet another cool way to use keywords:

1. Click the browser bar text field at the top of your screen.

2. Type the keyword into the browser bar text field.

3. Click Go.

See also "Getting a List of Keywords" in this part.

Part III

Chatting with Everyone

The heart of America Online beats with interactive discussion and chatter. Wherever people congregate to discuss issues, lifestyles, or interests, cyberspace flutters with activity. Join the fray! This part tells you how to locate online friends and engage in live talk in the chat rooms.

In this part . . .

Chats Run by AOL Protocol 38
Chat Room Fonts and Formatting 38
Chatting on AOL 38
Creating a Buddy Chat Room 39
Creating a Member Chat Room 39
Creating a Private Chat Room 40
Creating a Profile 41
Expressing Yourself in a Chat Room 41
Finding Chat Rooms 42
Finding Your Favorite Community 43
Getting Help in a Chat Room 44
Going to a Friend's Chat Room 44
Locating Someone on America Online 46
People Connection 46
Playing Sounds in a Chat Room 47
Reading Someone's Profile 47
Right-Clicking in Chat Rooms 48
Role-Playing Chat Rooms 48
Rolling Dice in a Chat Room 49
Using a Profile 49
Using Chat Rooms Safely 49

Chats Run by AOL Protocol

Many scheduled presentations use America Online Protocol, which adds a layer of complexity to the chat room but generally keeps things running smoothly. These chats often feature guest presenters, but they're scheduled in a regular service area chat room rather than one of the large arenas. When participating in a chat that uses protocol, follow these general guidelines:

✔ Wait until called upon to ask a question or voice a comment. The room host calls upon members by typing **GA** (for Go Ahead) and your screen name.

✔ Type and send ! (an exclamation point) to comment; then wait until recognized to type the comment itself.

✔ Type and send ? (a question mark) to ask a question but wait until the room host recognizes you before you send the question itself.

Using ! and ? in an organized chat is the equivalent of raising your hand if you were in an auditorium.

Chat Room Fonts and Formatting

Add flash to your chat room conversations with the chat room formatting bar. Perched above the text-entry field, the buttons on this bar enable you to change fonts (say, using Old English text to participate in a medieval role-playing game). Use the buttons next to the text field to change text color — or to bold, italicize, or underline your text. To add a special smile or frown to your words, the smiley button gives you a raft of emotions you can use to spice up your text — as if special colored text weren't enough. Selecting a special font and color for your contributions helps other chatters identify your text; too many varied colors and fonts, however, make the chat room window difficult to read.

Chatting on AOL

Chat rooms are the live-interaction areas of America Online. Most online forums use a chat room for interest-specific chats and presentations; the People Connection consists entirely of chat rooms. People Connection chat rooms are divided into categories. These categories are further split into *public rooms* created by America Online and *member rooms* created by AOL members.

Private chat rooms and *event arenas* are other options for America Online interaction. Anyone can create a private chat room to meet with friends. Large arenas (such as the Rotunda and the Coliseum) are reserved for scheduled presentations with guest speakers. *See also* "Finding Chat Rooms" in this part.

Creating a Buddy Chat Room

When you're tired of flipping Instant Messages (IMs) back and forth between your online friends, create a Buddy Chat room and include everyone in a private chat. Just follow these steps:

1. Click the Buddy Chat button at the bottom of the Buddy List window. The Buddy Chat dialog box opens, awaiting your instructions.

2. Enter the screen names that you want to invite in the Screen Names to Invite text box. The Buddy Chat window helpfully fills in any of your Buddy List friends who are currently online in the highlighted Buddy List. If you have other (or fewer) friends in mind, alter the list accordingly. If you invite the wrong group of friends, click Cancel at the bottom of the Buddy Chat screen and highlight another Buddy List in your Buddy List window before you click the Buddy Chat button.

3. Enter a room title (or the reason for getting together) in the Message to Send text box.

4. America Online suggests a name for the private chat room. Because you're dealing with a computer, the name is generally computeresque, like JSKaufeld15. If you prefer a more poetic room name, highlight the America Online choice and type your own suggestion.

5. Click Send. Your invitation wings its way to your guest list.

6. When you see your copy of the invitation appear, click Go to drop into your private chat room creation.

See also "Creating a Private Chat Room" later in this part.

Creating a Member Chat Room

Create a member chat room and discuss a favorite interest — live. Here's how:

1. Choose People➪Start Your Own Chat. The Start Your Own Chat dialog box appears, awaiting your instructions.

2. Click the Member Chat button. The Create a Member Room window jumps to the screen.

3. Select a category for your chat room. Then type in a name for the new room and click Go Chat — and you land in your newly created chat room. (Now if someone *else* would just show up!)

Creating a Private Chat Room

To talk privately with someone (or a group of someones), create a private chat room. Here's how:

1. Choose People⇔Start Your Own Chat. The Start Your Own Chat dialog box appears.

2. Click the Private Chat button to bring the Private Chat dialog box to the screen.

3. Enter a name for your new private room and click Go Chat. You zoom off to the new private domain.

When you create a private chat room, keep the following in mind:

✔ **Make the chat room name unique:** Don't be surprised if people drop into your private room every now and then because they accidentally thought up the same name that you did.

✔ **Be sure to give your invitees the right information:** Make sure everyone who wants to join you knows the room's name and the correct spelling. Otherwise, they create another private room and sit there all alone.

Want to meet some new people? Create a private chat room called *hello* or *chat* and see who shows up! You might be amazed at how little time you spend sitting in an empty private chat room.

Keyword **Private Chat** opens the Private Chat dialog box without any fuss. Type your chat room name into the text field and click the Go Chat button to be on your way.

See also "Chatting on AOL" and "Creating a Buddy Chat Room" elsewhere in this part.

Creating a Profile

Profiles identify America Online members. The profile is also your listing in the Member Directory.

Make your profile information appropriate for the screen name. For a general profile, tell people about your hobbies, occupation, and favorite quote. If you use a screen name strictly for business, include information about your company. If you play online simulation or role-playing games, describe your character. When you get right down to it, your profile is whatever you want it to be.

To create a profile of your own:

1. Use keyword **Profile** to open the Member Directory window.

2. Click the My Profile button. The Edit Your Online Profile window appears, covered by a large warning dialog box.

3. Click OK to make the dialog box go away.

4. Fill in the information that you want to share with the world, and click the Update button. In a few moments, your completed profile takes its place among the ranks.

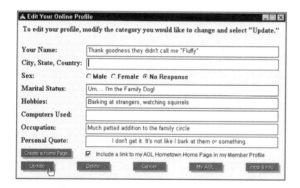

See also "Reading Someone's Profile" in this part, and Part IV for more on profiles.

Expressing Yourself in a Chat Room

How do you convey emotion and facial expressions in an all-text medium? The Internet pioneers had that same problem — and thus began the character-based symbols known as *emoticons* or *smileys*. If you've seen characters in a chat room like :) (a smile) or { { } } (virtual hugs) but never really understood what they meant, you can find a list of popular emoticons in Part V.

Along the same lines, you can't hang out for long in the chat rooms without seeing shorthand such as *AFK* or *LOL* scrolling across the screen. You're not watching an apoplectic typist; rather, these letters are abbreviations for commonly used terms. Away From Keyboard (AFK) and Laughing Out Loud (LOL) are two of the abbreviations developed by busy keyboardists. Because such abbreviations have their roots in e-mail, you can find more of them listed in Part V.

Finding Chat Rooms

Sometimes, locating online chat rooms is a bit more art than science. This section gives you the lowdown on locating all kinds of chats online: organized chats, member-created chat rooms, and chats that belong to individual online areas.

Most chat rooms on America Online wait patiently until located. Find a chat room in one of several ways:

✔ Use keyword **Chat Schedule** to open the AOL Chat Schedule window. This window lists system-wide chats for the week, hour by hour. Click a topic's button to see what chats fill the schedule. Some chats occur in various online areas; others are part of the regular People Connection roster.

✔ Choose People➪Find a Chat. Select a chat category that looks interesting. When you double-click a category, its chat rooms appear in the item list box to the right of the category list. Click one of the chat rooms in the list box to highlight it and then click Go Chat to land in that particular chat room

If none of the public rooms in the Find a Chat window (choose People➪Find a Chat) interest you, click the Created by AOL Members button to change the item lists. Now, only rooms created by members appear in the lists. Double-click a category to see its rooms. Highlight a room name, click the Go Chat button, and America Online sends you to that room.

✔ Go through AOL Live (keyword **AOL Live**) to see what's coming up in the celebrity and news chat scene. Click the Coming Soon button or browse through the Live Today list box to view the upcoming presentations. Click an item that looks interesting to find out more about it.

If you miss a chat, browse through AOL Live to download the transcript. Use the Event Transcripts button on the AOL Live window to reach the AOL Live Transcripts window. It's the next best thing to attending!

Finding Your Favorite Community

People Connection Communities bring people together for chat, discussions, information, and much more. Every AOL channel except Kids Only (which is one big community already), Teens, and Shopping offer a Community where you can meet others who share similar interests.

With the People Connection Communities, AOL takes the best of the old Forum windows and reworks them into a format that fits today's savvy surfer. Links in each Community page lead to related member home pages, chats, message boards, and featured topic areas. You can also link to related communities nestled under larger headings: A trip to the Learning Community, for instance, offers you other Communities that focus on space, history, homework, and the Civil War.

To locate the Community that features what you love:

✔ Click the Chat button on the Toolbar, and then select your favorite Community topic from the drop-down scroll box.

✔ Use the keyword for the particular Community that you want to see. Most of the Communities use the channel name with Community tacked onto the end, as in keyword **Learning Community** or keyword **Computing Community**.

✔ Keyword **Communities** takes you to the general People Connection window where you can select communities by topic from the drop-down scroll box.

Getting Help in a Chat Room

For general help about life in the People Connection, click the Help button in the upper right-hand corner of the chat room screen. If someone's being obnoxious, click the Notify AOL button in the lower right-hand corner of the chat window.

See also "Using Chat Rooms Safely" later in this part.

Going to a Friend's Chat Room

Friends hide in the most unlikely places, but joining them is easy if they're hanging out in a chat room. If the friend is part of a Buddy List Group, follow these steps:

1. Click the member's name in your Buddy List window. *See also* Part IV for the lowdown on Buddy Lists.

2. Click the Buddy Info button at the bottom of the window. An Info for *screen name* dialog box (where *screen name* is whom you're searching for) leaps to life offering you all sorts of information options. The dialog box also helpfully tells you that your buddy is online — but if her screen name shows in your Buddy List, you already knew that.

3. Click the Locate Buddy button at the bottom of the dialog box. America Online looks for your friend and gives you a report in the Locate *screen name* dialog box. If the member is in a chat room, the dialog box gives the name of the chat room.

4. Click Go to leap directly into the chat room.

If your friend's screen name is mysteriously missing from your Buddy List Groups, find her online this way:

1. Choose People⇨Locate Member Online. You see the Locate Member Online dialog box.

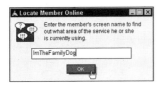

2. Type the member's screen name into the text field and then press Enter. If your friend inhabits a chat room, the Locate *screen name* dialog box tells you where she's hiding.

3. Click Go to join your friend in the chat room.

The Locate feature may reveal that your friend is in a private room. In that case, send an Instant Message (IM) to find out the name of the room. Of course, the person may respond that he's in a private room and you can't come . . . so there! But if he's a true friend, he gives you the name of the private room. After you know the room name, joining him there is easy. To join your friend, follow these steps:

1. Choose People⇨Start Your Own Chat to bring the Start Your Own Chat dialog box into view.

2. Click the Private Chat button. The Private Chat dialog box appears.

3. Enter the chat room name into the Private Chat dialog box and click Go Chat to join the private fun.

Locating Someone on America Online

Looking for someone? Try using the Member Directory to search for the person's name or screen name. If the person created a Profile, then the member's information is indexed in the Member Directory. If the person doesn't have a Profile entry, you can't find the name by searching the Directory — in fact, you probably can't find it at all.

If the person you find through the Member Directory is currently online, a small red triangle appears next to his name in the Member Directory Search Results window. Double-click any entry in the window to see that member's profile, and then use the Locate button in the Member Profile window to see whether she's currently in a chat room.

 If you already know the person's screen name and you simply want to locate them, choose People⇨Locate Member Online, enter your friend's screen name into the text box, and click OK. The system tells you whether your friend is currently online and whether he's in a public chat room.

See also "Searching the Member Directory" in Part IV and "Going to a Friend's Chat Room" in this part.

People Connection

People Connection is the doorway to interactive chats with America Online members around the world. To reach the People Connection screen, do one of the following:

✔ Click the Chat button at the bottom of the Welcome screen or on the toolbar.

✔ Choose People⇨Chat (People Connection).

✔ Use keyword **People Connection**.

Each of these actions takes you to the opening window of the People Connection screen. From there, use the buttons to navigate to the chat room of your choice. Choose from Find a Chat (which gives you a choice of chats by category), Chat Now (which drops you right into a general chat room), or Communities (a collection of special-interest groups from autos to spirituality).

See also "Chatting on AOL" and "Finding Chat Rooms" in this part.

Playing Sounds in a Chat Room

Noise livens life, so why not use it to add some spark to a chat room? In a chat room, type {S *soundname,* replacing *soundname* with the name of the sound. (By the way, you must use a capital S in the command; otherwise, it won't work. However, capitalization doesn't matter in the sound name.) Standard America Online sounds include *Welcome, Drop, IM, Gotmail,* and *Goodbye.*

To play any sound in your America Online folder or Windows directory, type the name of the sound file itself. For example, to play the sound POINK.WAV, type the command {S **poink**.

Playing too many sounds in a chat room gets annoying very fast, so use sounds sparingly.

Reading Someone's Profile

Profiles on America Online are members' portraits. They tell you as much or as little about a member as that person wants you to know. Some profiles are very specific, listing first and last names, occupations, and hobbies. Others are downright silly. (But that's what makes life fun.)

1. Choose People⇨Get AOL Member Profile. The Get a Member's Profile dialog box opens.

2. Enter the screen name of the member into the text box and click OK (or press Enter).

3. If the member has a profile, the Member Profile window opens. If no profile exists, a dialog box appears stating that no profile is available for a user by that name.

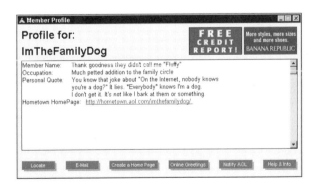

To locate the member online, use the Locate button at the bottom of the Member Profile window. To send an e-mail, click the E-Mail button. The Write Mail window leaps to the screen with the member's screen name already entered into the Send To text field.

Right-Clicking in Chat Rooms

Right-click in the chat room's text field to run a quick spell check before you send that reply (or to colorize your next line of text). A right-click in the chat room window selects all the text it contains.

Role-Playing Chat Rooms

Role-playing chat rooms operate a little differently than the general rooms. Check out keyword **People Games** and then click the Space Gaming, Free-Form, or Role-Playing buttons for more about this neat form of gaming. When participating in role-playing chat rooms, keep in mind the following general guidelines:

- Watch and listen before taking part. Get a feel for the game, the scenario, and what is and isn't proper. Play the game on its own terms.

- After you lurk (silently watch) a while, send an e-mail or an Instant Message to one of the players stating you'd like to play; then ask how to join. The recipient of your message should respond with particulars.

- Use a character (game persona) screen name. Playing in a room under a general name may get you some questioning Instant Messages.

- Create a specific profile for your character that tells other players what your character looks like, does for a living, and the like. Write the profile to describe your character instead of yourself.

- Use double colons (::) at the beginning and end of actions, as in **::walks into room and takes off cloak::**.

- Surround out-of-character comments with double parentheses: **((Do you really have blue hair??))**. Many simulations or role-play sessions request that you use Instant Messages for all out-of-character chatter.

- When switching between their comments and their characters' comments, some players use shorthand for In Character (IC) and Out of Character (OOC) to help everyone else know where they are. Some games ask that all out-of-character chatter take place in Instant Messages.

✔ Language requirements are very different in the role-playing games. Try to get a feel for what language is acceptable before you start to play.

Rolling Dice in a Chat Room

Lots of online games use dice rolls. To roll dice in a chat room, type **//roll-sides#-dice#** where the first # is the number of sides on the die and the second # is the number of dice rolled. Both number of sides and number of dice vary, depending upon the game.

For a quickie roll with a pair of six-sided dice, type **//roll** in the chat-room text box and click Send.

Using a Profile

When you meet people in a chat room and want to know a little more about them, take a peek at their profiles:

1. Choose People⇨Get AOL Member Profile. The Get a Member's Profile dialog box appears.

2. Type the member's screen name into the text box.

3. Click OK.

4. If available, the member's profile appears. If no profile exists for that screen name, a dialog box jumps to the screen to inform you.

If you happen to be in a chat room when the profile urge strikes, double-click any screen name in the member list to the right of the chat room window. A small Screen Name dialog box appears. Click the Get Profile button, and the profile appears if it's available.

Using Chat Rooms Safely

Chat rooms are great places to meet old and new friends, but you need to use common sense and logic when participating in a chat room. In the odd chance that you do come across any suspicious or offensive behavior, use these tools at your disposal.

Chat room Notify AOL button

Use the Chat Room Notify AOL button to report offensive chat and password solicitations. It rests in the lower right-hand corner of all chat room windows. Click the button to select the offending person's screen name and view the offensive chat text. Then click Send, and the report goes to the AOL Community Action Team. The team reviews the report and decides on appropriate action. Keyword **Notify AOL** also opens the Notify AOL window.

To report that someone requested your password, click the Notify AOL button at the bottom of the Instant Message Note window, enter any additional information the staff may need to know, and click the Send Report button.

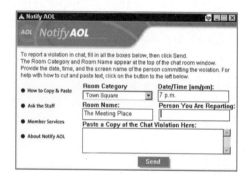

General chat room dos and don'ts

As with any place that hosts a gathering of people, chat rooms have their own protocol for what is and isn't proper. Sometimes etiquette differs among chat rooms, and the formality of a presentation alters etiquette as well.

The following are all-around etiquette guidelines for chat rooms:

- ✓ **DON'T SHOUT.** Typing in all caps is considered shouting and is generally frowned upon.

- ✓ **Refrain from vulgarity.** Not only is this a general rule of AOL etiquette, but it's also part of the Terms of Service (TOS). Swearing in a chat room can cause trouble.

- ✓ **Create a Member Profile for your screen name.** Profiles function as introductions in the online world, and other members like to see whom they're talking to. *See also* "Creating a Profile," and "Reading Someone's Profile" in this part.

✔ **Stick to the topic at hand.** If you visit a cooking chat room and begin a long, involved discussion about industrial rock music, other members may request that you return to the original topic or leave.

✔ **Feel free to question what people say in a chat room.** After all, conflict is the basis of many good discussions. Although you *can* question what folks say, you *can't* question their right to say it. The only exception to this is when someone violates the Terms of Service by swearing or being generally obnoxious.

Ignoring someone in a chat room

When someone in a chat room gets too obnoxious, ignore him. (It's the best form of revenge.) Here's how to ignore a person and make sure that none of his text appears in your chat window:

1. Double-click the obnoxious person's screen name in the People Here list. (The People Here list is the list of names on the right side of the chat room window.)

2. When the dialog box pops up, check the Ignore Member box.

3. Close the dialog box.

Repeat the steps to stop ignoring someone (assuming that he repented of his crime).

Reporting problems in a chat room

Occasionally in a chat room, you run into someone who just won't play by the rules. The person may use foul language, fill up the screen by continually sending irrelevant messages (such as *I exist!*), or just be downright obnoxious. (Keyword **TOS** gives you the lowdown on the dos and don'ts.)

Before doing anything else, ask the person to stop. If the person persists, follow these steps:

1. Highlight the offending text and use Edit⇨Copy to copy it.

2. Click the Notify AOL button at the bottom right-hand corner of the chat room screen. (It's the second button in the right column.) The Notify AOL window opens, with the chat room text already filled in.

3. Select the screen name of the offending person in Step 1 of the Notify AOL window.

4. Add any comments you want to clarify the situation in Step 2 of the Notify AOL window.

5. Click the Send button at the bottom of the window.

Remember: The Notify AOL button doesn't appear if you're in a private chat room. Remember that you went there on your own; if you don't like the things going on in that chat room, then close the window.

Part IV

IM Your Buddy, Locate Your Pal

With an America Online account, you're never alone. You can easily find your online friends and track their comings and goings so that you know when they're available to discuss life (and last night's game results). This part tells you how to locate online friends and chat one-on-one with Instant Messages.

In this part . . .

Adding a Buddy to Your Buddy List 54

Adding a Buddy to Your Address Book 54

Adding Links to Instant Messages 54

Buddy Lists 55

Changing a Buddy List Group 56

Creating and Using Away Messages 56

Creating a Buddy Chat Room 57

Creating a Buddy List Group 59

Deleting a Buddy List Group 59

Formatting Instant Messages 60

Getting Info about Your Buddies 60

Instant Messages (IMs) 61

Reading Someone's Profile from the IM Window . . . 61

Receiving Instant Messages 61

Reporting Problems in an Instant Message 62

Searching the Member Directory 63

Sending Instant Messages 65

Setting Buddy List Preferences 65

Adding a Buddy to Your Buddy List

After you successfully create a Buddy List, it sits waiting for you to fill it. Pack it with all the friends you can manage and keep track of each one. Here's how:

1. Use keyword **Buddy** to open the Buddy List window.

2. Click the Setup button to open the Buddy List Setup window.

3. Highlight the group name that you want to fill with buddies.

4. Click the Add Buddy button.

5. Type your buddy's screen name into the Add New Buddy dialog box and then click Save.

6. Your new buddy proudly takes her place in the group.

Adding a Buddy to Your Address Book

Sometimes, talking to your friends while online isn't enough. You may want to send them e-mail messages sometimes, too. Adding one or more Buddies to your Address Book is easy when you use the Buddy List window to do most of the work for you. Here's what you do:

1. While your friend is online, click his screen name in the Buddy List window to highlight it.

2. Click the Get Info button at the bottom of the Buddy List window. The Info for screen name dialog box opens.

3. Click the button next to Add to my Address Book. The Address Book Contact Details window opens, with your buddy's screen name already entered.

4. Fill in the person's name and any other details you want to keep in mind.

5. Click Save when you're done. The information takes its place in your Address Book list.

Adding Links to Instant Messages

To send a friend the name of a really neat place you found on America Online or the Web, open an Instant Message and drop a link to the area.

1. Open the area you want to tell your friend about.

2. Click the Favorite Places icon (the white rectangle with a red heart in the middle of it). A dialog box appears, asking what you want to do with the Favorite Place.

3. Click the Insert in Instant Message button. An Instant Message window opens with a blue-underlined title inserted. That's your link.

4. Type a description of the area into the message area of the Instant Message box.

5. Enter a screen name into the To text field.

6. Click the Send button.

To jump to the highlighted area link from an Instant Message, click the colored text. (Almost too easy, isn't it?)

Buddy Lists

America Online's Buddy List feature tells you when your friends sign on and off the service. Create groups to reflect how you use your AOL account and how you run your life: AOL gives you Buddy List Groups called Buddies, Family, and Co-Workers. If you organize your life around Online Gaming Buddies, Cooking Co-op, and Ongoing Projects instead, then set up your Buddy List to reflect that.

You can use your Buddy List to send Instant Messages, create a private chat room, or filter the people who can find you online. Also use the Buddy List Away Message to let other members know when you step away from your computer.

See also "Using an Away Message," "Setting Buddy List Preferences," "Creating a Buddy List Group," and "Sending Instant Messages" elsewhere in this part.

Changing a Buddy List Group

Sometimes your Buddy List Group needs a little tweaking to stay current. You can alter someone's screen name, Internet e-mail address, or Buddy List name after creating the Buddy List. Here's how:

1. Use keyword **Buddy** to open the Buddy List window.

2. Click the Setup button in the Buddy List window to open the Buddy List Setup window.

3. Click to highlight the list entry that you want to change.

4. The Buddy List Setup window gives you several options:

   • **To change the Buddy List Group name:** Click the Rename button and type a new name into the Rename text box. Click Save.

   • **To remove a screen name or Group from the list:** Click the Remove button. Click Yes to confirm that you truly want to delete this item.

   • **To add a screen name to the Buddy List:** Click the Add Buddy button and then type the name into the Enter New Buddy's Screen Name text field. Click Save.

5. When everything looks correct, click the Close box in the Buddy List Setup window.

See also "Creating a Buddy List Group" and "Deleting a Buddy List Group" in this part.

Creating and Using Away Messages

Lunch and dinner wait for no one. When mealtime calls or you need to take a quick break to grab another soda, create an Away Message for the occasion and then run your errand, secure in the knowledge that visiting friends know you'll return soon. An Away Message can be as useful or esoteric as you like, but Terms of Service (TOS) guidelines still apply.

Creating an Away Message

Before you use an Away Message, you need to create it. To create an Away Message:

1. Click the Away Message button in the Buddy List window. A menu appears to the left of the Buddy List window.

2. Click the Set Up Away Messages button. The Set Up Away Messages dialog box jumps to the screen.

3. Click the New button. The New Away Message window appears.

4. Type your message into the larger Enter New Message text window, and then give your message a title. AOL helpfully suggests names like *New Away Message 1*; if you think of something more creative, by all means use it.

5. Click Save to record your new Away Message.

Using an Away Message

Set up your Buddy List to respond to stray IMs while you're away from your computer. Create your own Away Message that explains that you're feeding the cat to the fish, or select from one of the pre-written Away Messages that America Online provides. To create and use a Buddy List Away Message:

1. Use keyword **Buddy** to open the Buddy List window if it doesn't already appear in the upper-right corner of your screen.

2. Click the Away Message button.

3. Click the New button in the Away Message window.

4. Type a descriptive title into the Enter Title text box. *Lunchtime* or *Feeding the Cat* are better titles than *New Away Message Number 1*. If you go to all the trouble to create an Away Message, you want to remember what it says the next time that you use it.

5. Type your message into the Enter New Message text box. When you're satisfied with your message, click Save.

6. To use your new message — or any message in the list — highlight the message in the Away Message window and click OK. The phrase Away Message On appears at the top of your Buddy List window, and anyone who sends you an Instant Message receives your Away Message as a reply.

 To turn off the Away Message, click the Away Message button. A small Away Message Off dialog box appears, telling you how long the Away Message was on and the number of IMs you received while it was active.

Creating a Buddy Chat Room

When you're tired of flipping Instant Messages (IMs) back and forth between your online friends, create a Buddy Chat room and include everyone in a private chat. Just follow these steps:

1. Click the Buddy Chat button at the bottom of the Buddy List window. The Buddy Chat dialog box opens, awaiting your instructions.

2. Enter the screen names that you want to invite in the Screen Names to Invite text box. The Buddy Chat window helpfully fills in any of your Buddy List friends who are currently online in the highlighted Buddy List. If you have other (or fewer) friends in mind, alter the list accordingly. If you invite the wrong group of friends, click Cancel at the bottom of the Buddy Chat screen and highlight another Buddy List in your Buddy List window before you click the Buddy Chat button.

3. Enter a room title (or the reason for getting together) in the Message To Send text box.

4. America Online suggests a name for the private chat room. Because you're dealing with a computer, the name is generally computeresque, such as JSKaufeld6. If you prefer a more poetic room name, highlight the America Online choice and type your own suggestion.

5. Click Send. Your invitation wings its way to your guest list.

6. When you see your copy of the invitation appear, click Go to drop into your private chat room creation.

Check out the Add Another Buddy to this Conversation button at the bottom of the Instant Message window. When you click it, the system opens a Buddy Chat invitation window, although Instant Messages still hold only two talkers at a time.

See also Part III for more on creating a private chat room.

Creating a Buddy List Group

Use a Buddy List Group to find your friends while they sign on to America Online (keyword **Buddy**). This list window appears when you sign on to the service, and you can set it to notify you when your online buddies sign on. You can also set a Buddy List Group preference to keep certain screen names from locating you with their Buddy List Groups. Here's how to create one:

1. Use keyword **Buddy**. The Buddy List window appears.

2. Click the Setup button. The Buddy List Setup window appears.

3. Click the Add Group button. The Add New Group window opens.

4. Type a catchall name for this Buddy List Group, such as **Work Pals** or **Friends;** then click Save.

Deleting a Buddy List Group

When you're fresh out of buddies, delete the Buddy List Group.

1. Use keyword **Buddy** to open the Buddy List window.

2. Click the Setup button to open the Buddy List Setup window.

3. Highlight the doomed group name in the Buddy List Setup window. (You can delete any Buddy List Group this way — even the default groups that AOL provides to start you off.)

4. Click the Remove button at the bottom of the window.

5. A dialog box appears and asks whether you're sure. Click Yes. The list is outta there.

See also "Creating a Buddy List Group" and "Changing a Buddy List Group" in this part.

Formatting Instant Messages

Use the buttons in the Instant Message window to make your IMs look like professional documents. Located at the top of the message text box, these nine buttons perform almost the same tasks as the e-mail formatting buttons. To use the buttons to format IMs, click the appropriate button before typing text. Or highlight text after typing and then click the desired button.

 Add emotion to your IM by clicking the last button in the lineup. This smiley face drop-down list gives you a range of expressions to choose from. So when you feel like smiling, frowning, or stating that your lips are sealed, select a face to say it for you.

Getting Info about Your Buddies

When you want to know more about one of your online buddies or you want to track down a buddy online, use the Buddy Info button at the bottom of the Buddy List window. Here's how:

1. Highlight your Buddy's screen name in the Buddy List window.

2. Click the Buddy Info button. The Info For *screen name* (where screen name is your Buddy's name) dialog box appears.

At this point, you have several options. You can:

- Send Mail to your Buddy.
- Send an Instant Message.
- Add your Buddy to your Address Book.
- View the Buddy's profile.
- View your friend's Web page.
- Locate your Buddy.

3. Click the button next to your choice and you're on your way.

Instant Messages (1Ms)

Communicate privately and individually with online friends through *Instant Messages.* These little windows appear in the top left-hand side of your screen. Instant Messages enable you to drop someone a quick question or comment if she's online — or talk privately with another member while sharing a public chat room.

See also "Receiving Instant Messages," "Sending Instant Messages," and "Reporting Problems in an Instant Message" later in this part.

Reading Someone's Profile from the 1M Window

Every now and then, you'd like to know a little more about the person you just spent an hour with chatting via Instant Message. When you get that sudden urge for more information, use the Buddy Info button in the IM window, and then click View Profile in the dialog box that appears. One click of the button, and your IM partner's profile leaps into view — that is, if he created a member profile in the first place.

Receiving Instant Messages

Sometimes an Instant Message appears on your computer screen, especially if you're cruising the chat rooms or several people have you in their Buddy List Groups.

1. When you receive an Instant Message, a small window pops into the upper left-hand corner of the screen.

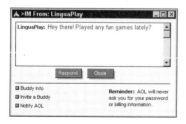

2. Click the Respond button. A duplicate text box appears at the bottom of the Instant Message window.

3. Type your response into the lower window, using the format buttons to spice up the text.

4. Click the Send button. Your response jumps to the top text box of the Instant Message window so that the original sender can read it.

If you decide you don't want to respond to the Instant Message, click Cancel or simply close the window by clicking the Close box.

Reporting Problems in an Instant Message

Offensive Instant Message senders take two forms: password scammers who want your account information or credit card number, or those folks who are just plain offensive. Sometimes, if you ask politely, the members sending you offensive messages will either stop and become polite or go away and leave you alone.

Someone asks for your password or credit card

During your America Online adventures, you might get an Instant Message or e-mail requesting your password or credit card information. Although these scamsters generally try to make you believe that they're from America Online, they're not. America Online would *never* need to contact you about your billing information or password. If anyone asks for that kind of information and then tells you he's from AOL, he's lying.

If you're in a chat room or cruising the online areas when you receive an Instant Message soliciting your password or credit card number, report the violation by following these steps:

1. Click the Notify AOL button at the bottom of the Instant Message window. A small Notify AOL dialog box appears.

Notify AOL

Instant Message Report to C.A.T.

Thank you for reporting a possible Terms of Service violation to the AOL Community Action Team (C.A.T.).

The text from the Instant Message in question will automatically be included in your report. If you wish to provide additional comments, please do so in the text box below.

When you are finished, click on the "Send Report" button.

Send Report   Cancel

2. Write any extra details that you think may be important into the text field of the dialog box.

3. Click Send Report. A copy of your Instant Message text, plus any extra information you provided, wings its way to the America Online Community Action Team.

If you decide you don't want to report the offense for some reason, click the Cancel button at the bottom of the Notify AOL dialog box. If your Instant Message window lacks a Notify AOL button, use keyword **Notify AOL** and then click the Instant Message button and follow the steps at the top of this section.

Someone acts generally obnoxious and annoying

Sometimes, people who send Instant Messages violate AOL's Terms of Service (TOS) by harassing other AOL members and using profanity. To report this type of Instant Message problems, follow these steps:

1. Click the Notify AOL button at the bottom of the Instant Message window. A small Notify AOL dialog box appears.

2. Enter any helpful information into the text box in the Notify AOL window . . . or leave it completely blank. Either way, your Instant Message violation report goes to the proper authorities.

3. Click Send Report. The Instant Message text and any additional text you entered into the Notify AOL text box goes to the Community Action Team, those friendly people responsible for following up violation reports.

Before calling in the America Online Community cops, nicely ask the annoying person to stop bothering you. If he keeps doing it, go ahead and report the lout.

Searching the Member Directory

You can search the Member Directory to find people who share your interests. To find the Member Directory window, do one of the following:

✔ Choose People➪Member Directory.

✔ Click the Member Directory button on any chat room window.

✔ Use keyword **Member Directory**.

After you reach the Member Directory window, focus on the options.

If you're looking for specific answers to individual fields in the Member Profiles (such as single men who use Macintosh computers and have chosen "To be or not to be" as a personal quote), choose the Advanced Search tab and fill in the appropriate fields. If you're just out for a quick search, the aptly named Quick Search tab should suit you fine.

1. Type whatever you're looking for (screen name, hobby, age, or whatever) in the Search Entire Profile for the Following Words text box.

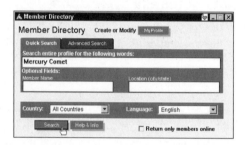

2. If you know the name of the person you're looking for, or if you're looking for someone who lives in a certain city or state, fill in the optional Member Name and Location fields.

3. Select a country from the pull-down list next to Country if you want to find a member from a particular country that America Online serves. Otherwise, leave the selection set to All Countries.

4. Click Search.

The search engine returns only a maximum of 100 results. If a topic matches 18,000 entries in the database, the search directory still returns only 100. So narrow your topic as much as you can when you start your search. For example, "Mercury Comet" as a search criterion returns a more focused group than "Cars."

If you're looking for someone with a common name, include an interest, occupation, or place of residence to narrow your search.

See John Kaufeld's *America Online 7.0 For Dummies,* published by Hungry Minds, Inc. for in-depth information on using the Member Directory to its fullest.

Sending Instant Messages

When one of your buddies appears online, you can send a cheery Instant Message to say hello using three different methods. To send an Instant Message:

⌐ Highlight a buddy's screen name in the Buddy List window and then click the Send IM button in the Buddy List window.

⌐ Choose People⇨Send Instant Message.

⌐ Click the IM button on the toolbar.

When the Send Instant Message window appears on screen, type the person's screen name into the To text field (unless it's already filled in). Then enter your message into the large text box in the bottom of the window and click the Send button. The Instant Message window disappears and re-opens in the top left-hand corner of your screen.

Setting Buddy List Preferences

Set your Buddy List to include certain people, exclude others, or exclude everyone (on those days when you *really* want to be alone). Also use your Buddy List Preferences to include a cute little icon in the Instant Message window that tells a little about you. To set your Buddy List Preferences:

1. Use keyword **Buddy** to open the Buddy List window if it's not already open.

2. Click the Setup button at the bottom of the Buddy List window.

3. Click the Preferences button to open the Buddy List Preferences window.

4. Alter any of the preferences and click Save to close the Buddy List Preferences window.

The Buddy List Preferences window offers lots of options. The window itself is divided into three tabs: Buddy List, Instant Messages, and Privacy. If you want to hear when your buddies arrive and leave, make sure the *Play sound when buddies sign-on* and *Play sound when buddies sign-off* check boxes are marked. Look for them under the Buddy List tab.

Under the Instant Messages tab, you can elect to timestamp your IMs; display the smilies you (and others) type into the IM window as art; use your Address Book to auto-suggest screen names for

your IMs; and display icons in the lower left-hand corner of the IM
window when you chat with someone who selected one of the IM
icons for their own account. With over 100 icons to choose from,
you're sure to find one that represents your personality — or something you love. To select an IM icon:

1. Look under the Instant Messages tab in the Buddy List
   Preferences window and choose the icon you want from the
   list. Click the Next button to see more icons if the first few fail
   to thrill you.

2. Click an icon to select it.

3. Click the Apply button to make the icon yours.

4. Click the Save button to set your changes and close the Buddy
   List Preferences window.

Use the Privacy tab to allow anyone to see you on their Buddy Lists
and contact you via Instant Messages, allow no one to find you
online, or settle on a level that falls between the two. Any privacy
settings can apply to either your Buddy List alone or your Buddy
List and Instant Messages. Click the button in front of the feature(s)
that you want to reflect the new privacy settings.

With the Buddy List and Instant Message privacy features, you can
elect to block — or allow — only the members whose screen
names you list in the text box. This feature gives you control over
those few annoying people in your world.

Expressing Yourself with E-Mail

Each America Online screen name comes with its own electronic mail, or e-mail, account. Possibly the most frequently used feature on the service, you can use e-mail to keep up with friends, stay in touch with family, and organize business communications. Revive the lost art of letter writing in a virtual way!

In this part . . .

AOL Address Book 68

Attaching a File to an E-Mail Message 70

Automatic AOL 72

Checking E-Mail Status 74

Copying Others with CC/BCC 75

E-Mail: Undeliverable, Deleting, Signatures 76

E-Mail: Etiquette, Expressing Yourself,
   Formatting, Reading 80

Receiving Official AOL Mail 85

Receiving an Attached File in
   an E-Mail Message 85

Replying to an E-Mail Message 86

Saving and Sending E-Mail Messages 87

Setting Your E-Mail Preferences 89

Sharing Favorite Places in an E-Mail 89

Sorting E-Mail 90

Undeleting and Unsending E-Mail Messages 90

Using Automatic AOL 91

Using a Signature in E-Mail 91

What's Your E-Mail Address? 92

Writing an E-Mail Message 92

AOL Address Book

The online Address Book helps you to keep e-mail addresses, business contact information, and personal friends organized and useful. Use the Address Book to gather e-mail addresses that you use frequently, track business associates (including optional home and cellular phone numbers and work addresses), and note the birthdays and anniversaries of close friends.

Adding an Address Book entry

To create an Address Book entry, follow these steps:

1. Choose Mail⇨Address Book to open the Address Book window.

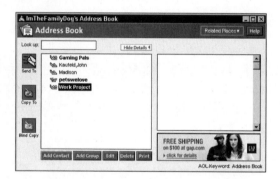

2. Click either the Add Contact or Add Group button to open the appropriate window. Add Contact creates an Address Book entry for an individual's screen name. Add Group creates a single Address Book entry for a group of screen names or Internet addresses, such as a list of family members who receive the annual Happy Holidays newsletter via e-mail.

- **In the Contact Details window:** Enter the person's first name, last name, and screen name or Internet address into the text boxes. Enter any further information you want to remember about that person, such as home address, work address, various phone numbers, or other personal details, into the fields under the corresponding tabs.

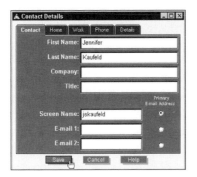

• **In the Manage Group window:** Enter a name for the group, such as Family, Friends, or Work Associates, into the *Create a name for your group* text box. Then enter the screen names or Internet addresses of the group's members into the large Additional Contacts in Group text box, or highlight the destined screen names in the Contact List text box and click Add.

3. The last option is *Do you want to share this group?* Clicking the Yes button launches you into creating a Groups@AOL Group. (*See* Part VI for more about the Groups@AOL feature.) Click No to keep your Group list strictly within your Address book.

4. Click Save. You now have a new contact or group of contacts in your Address Book.

The Address Book lives on the America Online servers — which means that every time you sign on, no matter what computer you use, AOL automatically updates your Address Book. So whether you use your AOL account at home, work, or both, your Address Book stays current.

Addressing e-mail with the Address Book

The Address Book remembers the e-mail addresses of your friends and associates. Use it to create mailing lists, to track names and e-mail addresses, or to do a little of both.

You actually can use this feature to create an entire contact file — complete with phone and fax numbers, business and home addresses, and more. Use as little or as much of the Address Book as you want — make it suit your needs and lifestyle.

See also "Adding an Address Book entry," "Changing or deleting an Address Book entry," and "Writing e-mail with the Address Book" elsewhere in this part.

Changing or deleting an Address Book entry

To change or remove an existing Address Book entry, follow these steps:

1. Click the name in your Address Book.

2. Click the Edit button to change the entry or click the Delete button to remove it.

- **Edit:** Click the Edit button to change the name or e-mail address of an entry. If you highlight a Personal entry, the Contact Details window pops to the screen. If you highlight a Group entry, the Manage Group window appears. Make any changes you want and then click Save to save the changes.

    If you highlight an entry in your Address Book that actually links to one of your Groups@AOL Groups, then clicking Edit does absolutely nothing.

- **Delete:** Click the Delete button to remove an entry from the Address Book. When a dialog box appears and asks whether you're sure, click Yes. The entry is toast.

 If the Address Book entry disappears without showing the dialog box and that bothers you, then set your Personal Filing Cabinet Preferences to confirm before it deletes single items.

See also "Adding an Address Book entry," earlier in this part, and Part VI for more information on Groups@AOL.

Attaching a File to an E-Mail Message

Use the Attachments button in the Write Mail window to send a file along with the e-mail message itself. The file then downloads into the receiver's computer.

To attach a file to an e-mail message, follow these steps:

1. Choose Mail⇨Write Mail, which opens the Write Mail window. (Or click the Write button on the toolbar.)

2. Click the Attachments button to open the Attachments window.

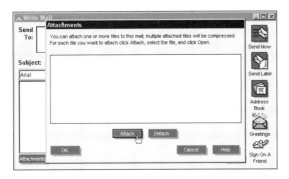

3. Click the Attach button to open the Attach window.

4. Type the name of the file you want to attach, or locate the name of the file in the list of files in the Attach window and double-click the filename. The filename appears in the Attachments dialog box.

5. If you want to attach only one file, click OK. The filename then appears under the Attachments button in the Write Mail window.

6. To attach a second (and subsequent) file, repeat Steps 3 and 4 until your file collection is ready to launch.

You can attach multiple files to an e-mail message. After you add a second file, AOL adds a comma to the filename under Attach. View your attached file list by clicking the Attachments button. If you like the attachment list, click OK. If you don't like the attachment list, use the Attach or Detach button in the Attachments window to modify the list until it satisfies you. Then click OK.

7. Fill in the e-mail address of the recipient and a subject to describe the e-mail message; then write a note in the message box explaining the attachment and click Send.

See also "Receiving an Attached File in an E-Mail Message," later in this part.

Automatic AOL

Automatic AOL automatically signs on to America Online and downloads your e-mail and files into your computer. You then read the e-mail offline, which cuts down on connect time and, in turn, saves you money if you subscribe to one of America Online's measured service options.

Find out more about Automatic AOL in *America Online 7.0 For Dummies,* by John Kaufeld (Hungry Minds, Inc.).

Before you can use Auto AOL, tell the America Online software what you want to do with it. Here's how:

1. Choose Mail⇨Automatic AOL. You do not need to be online to do this. The Automatic AOL Walkthrough window opens, giving you the option of choosing Expert Setup or Continue.

2. If you've set up your Automatic AOL before, click Expert Setup. Then click the boxes in front of the options to select or deselect them. If no options are selected, the Automatic AOL session runs but actually does nothing.

   If you've never set up an Automatic AOL before, click the Continue button. AOL walks you through the setup, describing each Automatic AOL option. Follow the instructions on-screen and click OK when you reach the Congratulations screen. You're done! Skip the rest of these directions and go straight to the upcoming "Using Automatic AOL" section.

3. Click the boxes in front of the tasks you want Auto AOL to perform. You can choose one or more of the following options:

   • **Send mail from the Mail Waiting to Be Sent folder:** This sends e-mail that you've written offline and saved to send later.

   • **Get unread mail and put it in Incoming Mail folder:** This option downloads all new, unread e-mail into your computer.

   • **Download files that are attached to unread mail:** Check this if you want America Online to download any files attached to e-mail messages at the same time it downloads the e-mail messages themselves. I leave this option unchecked and download all files manually if I decide I want them. It minimizes the chance of learning too late that you've downloaded a hacker file.

- **Send postings from the Postings Waiting to be Sent folder:** This option sends any newsgroup postings you may have written to their respective newsgroups.

- **Get unread postings and put in Incoming Postings folder:** America Online grabs the new postings from any newsgroups you subscribe to and downloads them into your computer.

- **Download files marked to be downloaded later:** Any files you found while roaming around America Online and for which you clicked the Download Later button will be copied into your computer if this box is checked. You'll find the files in the folder you designated for downloads under Download Preferences (keyword **Preferences**).

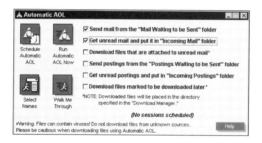

4. Click the Schedule Automatic AOL button to tell AOL when to download your e-mail. Check Enable Scheduler to activate the scheduling feature. If you don't want AOL to download files without your help, you can skip this section.

5. Click the Run Automatic AOL Now button to begin an Auto AOL session immediately. A small dialog box appears, asking whether you want the system to sign you off when the Automatic AOL session is finished. Check *Sign off when finished* if you're ready to leave America Online for a while and then click Begin. If you click the Begin button without checking the *Sign off when finished* box, the system downloads your e-mail and then awaits your next keyword or mouse click.

6. Click the Automatic AOL window's close box to save your changes and make the Automatic AOL dialog box go away.

If you want your computer to sign on to America Online automatically and download your e-mail, you have to store the passwords for the screen name(s) on your computer. To do that, click the Select Names button in the Automatic AOL window. The Select Screen Names dialog box appears. Check the boxes next to the screen name(s) that you want to use, and type the password next to the corresponding screen name(s). Click OK to save your changes or Cancel if you change your mind.

Storing your password in the Automatic AOL screen does *not* allow general access to your account. No one can get to your computer and sign on to America Online under your name. The password included here allows your computer to download your e-mail from America Online without your physical help.

If you go to the trouble of entering your password in the Select Names section, remember to use the Schedule Automatic AOL button to select the days and times for the Automatic AOL sessions. Check Enable Scheduler in the Schedule Automatic AOL dialog box, or your password entry work is for naught.

Checking E-Mail Status

Find out what your America Online e-mail correspondents actually *do* with your messages through the *e-mail status* option.

This option only works for mail sent to another America Online subscriber. If you try to check the status of an Internet e-mail message, the system reports that status checks are not applicable (you cannot check status of Internet mail).

1. Choose Mail⇔Read Mail, and then select Sent Mail from the pop-up menu that appears. The Mailbox window hops into view, proudly displaying the Sent Mail tab.

2. Click once on the message that you want to check; then click the Status button at the bottom of the window. A status window appears, showing the time and date the recipient read the message. If the recipient hasn't read the message yet, the status window reads (not yet read); if the message was deleted without having been read, the status window reads (deleted).

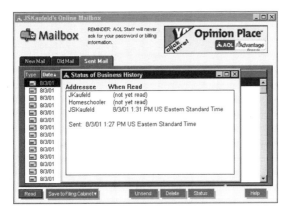

Copying Others with CC/BCC

Sending carbon copies (CC) or blind carbon copies (BCC) of e-mail messages to friends or colleagues is a snap on America Online. Here's how:

1. To send a carbon copy, type the screen name(s) or Internet address(es) into the Copy To text box on the right-hand side of the Write Mail screen.

2. To send a blind carbon copy, type the screen name(s) or address(es) in parentheses () in either the Send To text box or the Copy To text box.

3. Fill in the subject and message boxes and click the Send button.

When you use the BCC option, the original recipient of the e-mail message knows nothing of a carbon copy. A carbon-copied message lists the e-mail address of the additional recipient(s) at the top of the e-mail message, but a message with a blind carbon copy lists nothing. Use the BCC option carefully — some folks don't like that kind of secrecy.

See also "Writing an E-Mail Message," later in this part.

Creating an E-Mail Signature File

Before you can use a signature file in e-mail, you need to create one. To create an e-mail signature file, follow these steps:

1. Choose Mail⇨Mail Signatures from the toolbar.

2. Click the Create button in the Set Up Signatures window. The Create Signature dialog box opens.

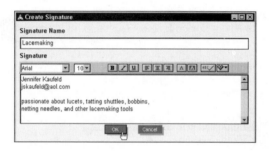

3. Type a name for your Signature into the Signature Name text field that best describes its purpose, such as Business, Pet Sitting, or Lacemaking.

4. In the Signature text box, include your contact information and anything else you want readers to know. You might want to include some or all of the following information:

- **Your name** — which is, after all, the point of a signature file. You can use just your first name or both your first and last names.

- **Your e-mail address** so that other people can contact you.

- **A Web site hyperlink** to your Web page where people can find out more about you or about what you do.

- **A favorite quote** that describes your unique view of life.

- **A few sentences** that explain what you do or why you care about an issue important to you.

5. When you're finished, click OK to establish the signature file. The signature takes its place in the Set Up Signatures dialog box.

6. To create another signature (because you're on a roll), click the Create button and go through the entire process one more time.

7. To edit a signature in the Set Up Signatures window, highlight the signature and click the Edit button. Make your changes and then click OK.

See also "Dropping a Signature into Your E-Mail," later in this part.

Dealing with Undeliverable E-Mail

Every now and then, an e-mail message you sent shows up again in your mailbox. For some reason, the computers couldn't deliver it. Here are some possibilities:

✓ The e-mail address wasn't quite correct. Odds are that you misspelled part of the address (but don't feel bad — this happens to some of us all the time). Double-check the spelling and try again. If the message comes back one more time, call the recipient and verify the address. Maybe the recipient changed Internet service providers, screen names, or (yipes!) canceled her account altogether.

✓ The computer at the other end was asleep or simply didn't respond. Things like this happen sometimes when you send a message halfway across the world. Try re-sending it within the next few days.

✓ The e-mail address was a phony. This gets kind of tricky, but some junk e-mail messages come with fake From addresses. That way, tracking down the people sending you unwanted junk mail and telling them to take you off their list is a great deal harder.

Deleting an E-Mail Message

Annoyed by unwanted marketing junk mail? No problem — that's why America Online created the Delete button.

 After a message is deleted from your America Online mailbox, it's gone after 24 hours. Nothing can bring it back. If you're really, really sure you want to trash that spam, follow these steps:

1. Click the You've Got Mail icon on the left-hand side of the Welcome screen to open the Online Mailbox. If you're in a hurry, click the Read button on the toolbar.

2. Use the arrow keys or click the message name to highlight the message in the New Mail window.

3. Click the Delete button at the bottom of the Online Mailbox screen.

A similar process works for mail that you've previously read:

1. Choose Mail⇨Read Mail, and then select Old Mail from the pop-up menu that appears to open your Online Mailbox with the Old Mail tab's contents proudly displayed.

2. Use the arrow keys or click the message name to highlight the message in the Old Mail window.

3. Click the Delete button at the bottom of the Online Mailbox screen.

When you send an e-mail message, a copy remains in your outgoing mailbox at America Online. If you don't want the copy hanging around, go through these steps to delete it:

1. Click the Read button on the toolbar.

2. Click the Sent Mail tab.

3. Use the arrow keys or click the message name to highlight that message in the Sent Mail window.

4. Click the Delete button at the bottom of the Online Mailbox screen.

See also "Unsending E-Mail," and "Undeleting an E-Mail Message," later in this part.

Dropping a Signature into Your E-Mail

After you create a signature file, the next step is to actually use the signature in an e-mail message. America Online gives you two options for using signatures. You can either designate a default signature that drops into the Write Mail window each time you create a message, or you can select a signature individually when you want to use one.

To designate a default signature, follow these steps:

1. Choose Mail⇨Mail Signatures from the toolbar.

2. Click to highlight one of the signatures in your Signatures list.

3. Click the Default On/Off button to select that signature as your default e-mail signature. A check mark appears next to that signature, showing that it's the default.

4. Close the Set Up Signatures window by clicking the close
button in the top right-hand corner.

Whenever you click the Write button on the toolbar to open the
Write Mail window, your signature automatically appears in the
window.

Turn off the default signature by opening the Set Up Signatures
window, highlighting the checked signature, and clicking Default
On/Off. The check mark disappears, and the signature is no longer
marked as the default.

To switch between signatures, click to highlight any signature in the
list and then click the Default On/Off button. The check mark jumps
to the new signature filename, and it becomes your default signature.

To select a particular signature from the list, follow these steps:

1. Open the Write Mail window by clicking the Write button on
the toolbar.

2. If you already selected a signature as default, it appears in the
Write Mail window. Highlight that signature and press the
Delete button to make it go away.

3. On the text-formatting bar in the Write Mail window, click the
last button, which looks like a pencil. A drop-down list displays
your current signatures.

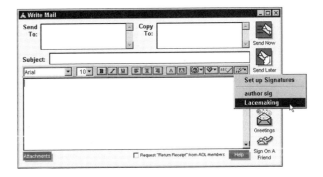

4. Select a signature from the list, and it appears in the Write Mail
window.

5. Type your message at the cursor, which appears in the blank
line above the signature.

6. Enter an e-mail address and a subject and then click the Send
Now button. The message leaves for its appointed destination.

See also "Creating an E-Mail Signature File," earlier in this part.

E-Mail Etiquette

Electronic mail uses an etiquette all its own, and it differs from the etiquette of normal spoken or written language. Because e-mail messages are short and rely on text and pictures (not verbal inflection or body language), paying attention to e-mail manners helps avoid misunderstandings.

 ✔ **Proofread, proofread, proofread.** The recipient sees only words on a page; if those words are horribly misspelled, they create an impression about you, who you are, and what's important to you (which may not be what you intend).

 ✔ **Don't type everything in ALL CAPS because doing so makes your text LOOK LIKE YOU'RE SHOUTING.** You can use all capitals for emphasis sometimes but use them sparingly.

 ✔ **Avoid using Internet shorthand and emoticons, such as LOL (Laughing Out Loud) and ;), to help convey meaning.** Although these devices are quite acceptable for informal e-mail, avoid them in business messages (unless you're writing to Internet denizens).

 ✔ **Sign e-mail messages with your name and Internet e-mail address.** Your Internet e-mail address is your screen name with @aol.com tacked on to the end (as in jskaufeld@aol.com).

Expressing Yourself in E-Mail

Conveying a whole range of feelings, expressions, and other subtleties can be difficult when you're communicating via e-mail. To solve this problem, creative e-mailers around the world have devised methods of adding touches of humor, class, and personality to the otherwise dry text of electronic mail.

Emoticons {*}, ;)

These little symbols appear in e-mail messages, in chat rooms, in newsgroups — anywhere people communicate on America Online. If you see one you don't recognize, ask what it means. Most people are friendly enough to increase your symbol vocabulary.

Symbol	What It Means
:)	Smiling
:(	Frowning
:'(	Crying
;)	Wink

Symbol	What It Means
:D	Big smile
:P	Raspberries
{}	Hug
{{{}}}	Hugs
:*	Kiss
{*}	Hug and a kiss
_/	Bar drink
c(_)	Coffee mug
c|_|	Beer stein
@-}--	Rose

Keyboard shorthand

Spice up your e-mail with shorthand. Abbreviations, called *shorthand*, are used in e-mail messages, Instant Messages, and chat rooms on America Online to help communicate emotion. They also create a feeling of intimacy among the initiated. After you know what LOL (Laughing Out Loud) means, you tend to giggle along, too, when you see it. The following shorthand abbreviations get you started:

Abbreviation	What It Means
AFK	Away from keyboard
BAK	Back at keyboard
BFN	Bye for now
BRB	Be right back
BTW	By the way
DC	Disruptive chatter
DH	Dear husband
DW	Dear wife
FWIW	For what it's worth
GMTA	Great minds think alike
IMHO	In my humble opinion
LOL	Laughing out loud
ROFL	Rolling on floor laughing
TTFN	Ta-ta for now
WB	Welcome back
WTG	Way to go!

Formatting E-Mail

Fourteen buttons sit at the top of the Message text box in the Write Mail window. Use these buttons to format your e-mail message. In order from left to right, these buttons do the following:

- ✔ Change text font

- ✔ Change text size

- ✔ Bold text

- ✔ Italicize text

- ✔ Underline text

- ✔ Set left edge of text even with left margin

- ✔ Center text in the message box

- ✔ Set right edge of text even with right margin

- ✔ Change text color

- ✔ Change the message's background color

- ✔ Insert a graphics file image

- ✔ Insert a Favorite Place

- ✔ Check spelling

- ✔ Insert signature file

Right-clicking in the message text field brings a pull-down menu to your screen. From here you can add a hyperlink, insert a text file you've previously saved, or insert a background image into your message.

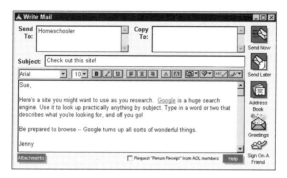

A hyperlink enables you to type the name of a really cool site you've found and include a link for it in your message; the recipient can simply click the site's name and open it on-screen. To create a hyperlink, follow these steps:

1. Right-click in the message field.

2. Choose Insert a Hyperlink. The Edit Hyperlink dialog box appears, waiting for your instructions.

3. Enter the name of the site into the Description field of the Edit Hyperlink dialog box.

4. Enter the Internet address into the Internet address field.

5. Click OK. The name you type into the Text field appears in the message box, dressed in underlined blue text.

If the hyperlink you want to include is already part of your Favorite Places list, click the purple heart above the text box in the Write Mail window and select from your Favorite Places assemblage. Click your choice and it drops into the e-mail message right at your cursor.

To format existing text in a message, click and drag across the text to highlight it; then click the buttons for the formatting you want. To mix and match formatting options, just click more than one button (to make text bold and italic, for example, click the Bold button and then the Italic button).

To format new text while you type it, click the format buttons that you want and then enter the text.

See also "Writing an E-Mail Message," later in this part.

Reading E-Mail

You miss out on an essential part of the online experience if you don't read the mail in your Online Mailbox. The following sections show you what you need to know.

Reading e-mail offline

To access your new mail anytime you want, read electronic mail offline. Here's how:

1. Use an Automatic AOL session to download unread e-mail.

2. Choose Mail⇨Filing Cabinet. The Filing Cabinet for your screen name appears with the Mail tab prominently displayed.

3. Look in the Incoming/Saved Mail folder for your downloaded mail messages.

4. To highlight the message, click it.

5. Double-click the highlighted message to open it or click Open.

Highlight the message in the Incoming/Saved Mail window and click the Delete button when you no longer need the e-mail. Remember, however, that after a message is deleted from the Filing Cabinet, it's gone for good.

See also "Automatic AOL," earlier in this part.

Reading e-mail online

When your account contains mail, America Online notifies you with a cheery You've Got Mail! announcement when you sign on. To read new mail, follow these steps:

1. Click the You've Got Mail icon on the Welcome screen.

Click the Read icon on the Toolbar to open your online mailbox quickly.

2. Use the mouse or arrow keys to move to the message you want to read.

3. Double-click the highlighted message or click the Read button at the bottom of the window. The e-mail message opens.

If you receive unwanted blanket advertising e-mail (also known as *spam*), e-mail with less than savory content, or a message requesting your AOL password or other private information, simply close the message and click the Notify AOL button at the bottom of the Online Mailbox window. In the Notify AOL dialog box that appears, either type an explanatory message into the text box or leave it blank, and click the Send Report button. The errant e-mail message wings its way to the AOL Community Action Team for review.

Receiving Official AOL Mail

If you receive an e-mail message that appears with a blue envelope in the New Mail list and sports a snazzy blue border in the message window itself, then you are the proud recipient of Official AOL Mail. Official AOL Mail comes to your mailbox courtesy of:

- ✔ E-mail from AOL's You've Got Pictures service

- ✔ Messages from founder Steve Case

- ✔ E-mail that announces a new screen name you created

- ✔ Welcome letters from AOL congratulating you on your new account

- ✔ Messages from AOL Official Mail itself

In time, all e-mail from AOL corporate (not specifically requested by members) will appear in the mailbox as Official AOL Mail.

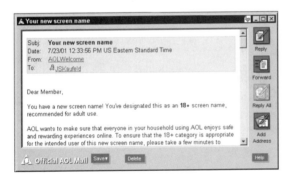

Receiving an Attached File in an E-Mail Message

If you open the listing for new mail and see a message with a small disk icon underneath the message icon, that message has an attachment of some kind. Document files, programs, and sound files are some of the attachments possible with e-mail. *See also* Part VIII for all the ins and outs of downloading e-mail attachments.

If you use Automatic AOL to download your mail and you previously checked the Automatic AOL preference labeled `Download files that are attached to unread mail`, the file is copied to your hard drive during the Auto AOL session. You still need to locate the file on your hard drive and open it, however. It will be waiting for you in the destination file listed in the Download Manager.

Replying to an E-Mail Message

Electronic-mail relationships last only if you write back. Respond to messages by following these steps:

1. With the original e-mail message open, click the Reply button. A new mail window appears with address and subject already filled in.

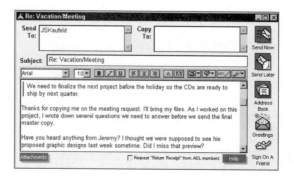

To include text from the original message in your reply, right-click anywhere inside the original message box, choose Select All from the pop-up menu that appears, and click the Reply button. A new mail window appears with the e-mail address and subject with Re: already filled in, as well as a complete copy of the message. Erase the parts that you don't want to send back; the blue line at the left side of the paragraphs that you want to keep from the original shows that those lines are quoted material.

If you want to quote only a small portion of the e-mail message, highlight that sentence or paragraph and then click the Reply button. The Reply Mail window opens with that portion of the message copied, complete with blue quotation line.

2. Type in your replies and comments.

3. Click the Send Now button to dispatch the message right away, or click the Send Later button to send it at a future time.

See also "Sending E-Mail," later in this part.

Saving Individual E-Mail Messages

On those days when you receive a gem or two in your e-mail box but you really don't want to download the entire morass into your Filing Cabinet with Automatic AOL, one button click allows you to save that special message. You can use this feature to organize your mail into folders in your Filing Cabinet. Here's how:

1. In the open Online Mailbox window, highlight the message that's too good to let go and click the Save to Filing Cabinet button.

2. A pop-up menu appears, giving you four choices. You can save the message to your general Mail folder, the Incoming/Saved Mail folder, or the Mail You've Sent folder. Or click the Create Folder button to create a completely new holding place for your special e-mail messages.

3. Select an option, and the mail drops into the folder. If you select Create Folder, the system prompts you for a folder name. The new folder then takes its place in the Save to Filing Cabinet lineup.

4. To view the saved message, choose Mail↪Filing Cabinet from the toolbar and open the Mail folder in the Mail tab.

The system drops the mail message into the folder each time that you select a folder. If you have some reason for wanting a message in three different places in the Filing Cabinet, you can do that.

Sending E-Mail

Sending e-mail messages and greetings may seem complicated, but the process is really quite simple. Read the following sections to find out how to send electronic greetings.

Sending an e-mail greeting card

Brighten a friend's day with a free e-mail greeting card. Whether you want to send holiday wishes, a thank-you note, remember a birthday, or celebrate a friendship, you'll find plenty to choose from at the American Greetings e-mail greeting card site (www.americangreetings.com).

To send an e-mail greeting card:

1. Click the Greetings button in an open Write Mail window, or use keyword **Mail Extras** to open the Greetings and Mail Extras window.

2. Click the Greetings button in the Greetings and Mail Extras window.

3. The American Greetings site opens, where you can select from hundreds of online greeting cards.

4. Select a card, fill in the recipient's e-mail address into the space provided, and click the Send button to forward your greeting.

Keyword **AG** takes you directly to the American Greetings site for those days when you're in a rush.

Sending e-mail to AOL members

To send an e- mail message to another America Online member, use the member's screen name in the Send To text field of the Write Mail window. E-mail sent from one AOL account to another requires only the member's screen name and not the @aol.com extension that you need for the Internet.

See also "Writing an E-Mail Message," later in this part.

Sending e-mail to several addresses

You can send electronic mail to several addresses at once instead of retyping the same message to several people. Type the addresses into the Send To field of the Write Mail window one after another, separating the addresses with commas.

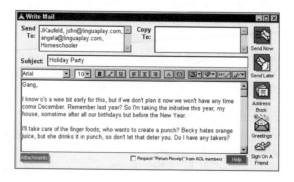

See also "Writing an E-Mail Message," later in this part.

Sending e-mail to people on the Internet

Sending an Internet e-mail message requires that you include the entire Internet address. Use the person's whole e-mail address, including the @whatever that comes after the name or account name. E-mail sent to other online services also needs the Internet extension, as in jkaufeld@juno.com. Enter the Internet address into the Send To field of the Write Mail window.

See also "Writing an E-Mail Message," later in this part.

Setting Your E-Mail Preferences

Choose from several electronic-mail preferences. Set preferences to save copies of incoming and outgoing mail automatically, use AOL style quotes in mail messages, and turn off the annoying Your Mail Has Been Sent dialog box.

See also Part I for information about these settings and many others.

Sharing Favorite Places in an E-Mail

To tell your friends about the latest cool Web page or America Online forum, send them an e-mail with a built-in hotlink to the site. Here's how:

1. Use the keyword or Web site address to open a window that contains the cool site you want to link in the message.

2. Click the Favorite Places icon on the window. It's the red heart on the white background. A small Favorite Place dialog box opens, telling you that you selected a Favorite Place.

3. Click the Insert in Mail button. A new e-mail window opens with the subject line already filled in and some blue underlined text in the window. That's the link!

4. Enter the person's screen name or Internet address and add any additional information in the Message text box.

5. Click the Send Now button.

When the recipient opens your mail message and clicks the blue hyperlink text, she goes directly to that site.

E-mail hotlinks are great for press releases promoting a Web site or an America Online service area.

To send a friend a Favorite Places link when you've already begun writing her a message, use the Insert Favorite Place button at the top of the message text box in the Write Mail window. It's the third button from the right. Click the button, and your Favorite Places list appears. Highlight the favorite place that you want to send, and America Online automatically inserts it into your mail message wherever your cursor rests. Pretty cool, eh?

Sorting E-Mail

Some days you want to see your mail in alphabetical order, other days you don't. Sort your mailbox contents to reflect the way you deal with messages: by date, sender's e-mail address, or subject line.

To sort the e-mail in your mailbox:

1. Open the Online Mailbox window by clicking the Read toolbar button.

2. Use the buttons at the top of the Online Mailbox window to sort the mail by Type, Date, Email Address, or Subject.

Sort your Sent Mail in descending order by e-mail address to avoid scrolling up and down the Sent Mail window for the second e-mail you sent to a particular address.

Undeleting an E-Mail Message

On those days when your fingers move faster than your brain and you delete some impressively important e-mail message, you no longer need to panic. Take a deep breath — fix yourself another cup of java if you want — and then undelete the e-mail you mistakenly toasted.

To undelete an e-mail message, follow these steps:

1. Choose Mail⇨Recently Deleted Mail from the toolbar. The Recently Deleted Mail window opens.

2. Highlight the wayward e-mail message by clicking it.

3. Click the Keep as New button.

4. The message takes its proper place in your New Mail window.

Use the Read button to look at the e-mail contents if you need to know exactly *which* message you want to resurrect. If you find one or two that you're *sure* you don't want, highlight them and click Permanently Delete. They're history.

Unsending E-Mail

Not every e-mail message should be sent to its intended recipient. If you write a message that makes you think twice after sending it, try *unsending* it. Here's how to unsend an e-mail message:

1. Click the Read button on the toolbar to open your Online Mailbox and then click the Sent Mail tab.

2. To highlight the message in question, click it.

3. Click the Unsend button at the bottom of the window. A dialog box appears asking whether you really want to unsend the message.

4. Click the Yes button in the dialog box. The message is unsent, and a small dialog box pops onto the screen with a terse `The message has been unsent` notification.

5. Click OK.

 Think fast — you can only unsend an e-mail up to the point that the person on the other end reads it. After that, you're stuck buying flowers or ice cream for the recipient.

Remember: This trick works only for unread sent messages to other America Online members. An e-mail message addressed to an Internet address cannot be unsent. (Choose your words wisely when they're headed for the Net.)

See also "Checking E-Mail Status," earlier in this part.

Using Automatic AOL

After you patiently set up the Automatic AOL information, it's time to watch Automatic AOL do its stuff. Follow these steps:

1. Choose Mail⇨Automatic AOL from the toolbar. The Automatic AOL dialog box pops up.

2. Click the Run Automatic AOL Now button to open the Run Automatic AOL Now dialog box.

3. Click Begin to start the Automatic AOL session.

See also "Automatic AOL," earlier in this part.

Using a Signature in E-Mail

Sign your e-mail messages with flair. Use a signature to personalize your e-mail closing without retyping lines of text each time you write a message. Best of all, you can create several different signature files to represent the various life roles you play: Create a different e-mail signature for your professional life, hobbies, family, and volunteer work.

In a signature file, you can include a link to your Web page or a brief description of your home business — here's where you "advertise" your wares if you want to let people know about your Web site or what you do for a living.

Like everything else that passes through the America Online portals, your signature file needs to follow TOS guidelines. So keep it clean or the TOS cops will find you in short order. For your own protection, an e-mail signature should include no home address, phone numbers, or other identifying information someone could use to find you.

See also "Creating an E-Mail Signature File," and "Dropping a Signature into Your E-Mail," both earlier in this part.

What's Your E-Mail Address?

Your Internet e-mail address is your America Online screen name. Put your AOL screen name in all-lowercase characters (the Internet ignores uppercase in mail addresses) and add @aol.com to the end. For example, my screen name is JSKaufeld, but my e-mail address is jskaufeld@aol.com.

Writing an E-Mail Message

There's more than one way to write an e-mail message. You can draft a message to send friends later, or you can send off a note while you're online. The following sections show you how.

Writing an e-mail message offline

If you use one of America Online's measured service options, writing messages offline saves money by shortening your connection time. When you compose e-mail messages offline, you can ponder word choices without watching the America Online clock tick or clicking the Yes button in the You've Been Idle — Do You Want to Stay Online? dialog box.

The process is nearly the same as the one I describe in "Writing an e-mail message online" later in this part. Meanwhile, here's how:

1. With the America Online software running but not connected by modem, choose Mail⇨Write Mail (or simply click the Write button) on the toolbar. The Write Mail window opens.

2. Enter the recipient's e-mail address in the Send To text box on the Write Mail window.

3. In the Subject text box below the address, enter a few descriptive words that tell the intent of the message. Press Tab to continue.

4. Write your message in the message text box.

5. When the message is complete, click the Send Later button at the right side of the window.

6. To send the message, sign on to America Online and begin an Automatic AOL session.

See also "Automatic AOL," and "Writing e-mail with the Address Book," elsewhere in this part.

Writing an e-mail message online

Electronic mail makes the Internet go 'round. To put your two cents' worth into the process, create your own e-mail messages and send them to friends and colleagues. To compose a message:

1. Choose Mail⇨Write Mail or click the Write toolbar button.

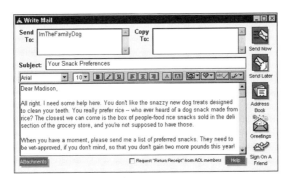

2. Enter the recipient's e-mail address in the Send To text box on the Write Mail window.

3. In the Subject text box below the address, enter a few descriptive words that tell the intent of the message. Keep in mind that a subject line such as Lunch Sunday tells more than Hello. Press Tab to continue.

4. Write your message in the message text box that takes up most of the Write Mail window.

5. Dress up your message with some text formatting. Use the buttons at the top of the message box to apply bold, italic, and other highlights to your text. Try clicking the camera icon and inserting an image to spice up your e-mail.

6. When you finish writing the message, click the Send Now button on the right-hand side of the Write Mail window. America Online immediately sends the e-mail to its destination.

If you have second thoughts after sending a message to an America Online member, *see also* "Unsending E-Mail," earlier in this part.

Right-click in the message text box to choose from several new mail features. Use the menu that appears to insert a background image, open and insert a saved text file, insert a regular image, or create a hyperlink to your favorite Web site.

See also "Sending E-Mail," earlier in this part.

Writing e-mail with the Address Book

To save time when writing e-mail messages, copy the address directly from the Address Book. Just follow these steps:

1. Open the Write Mail window.

2. Click the Address Book button on the right-hand side of the window.

3. When the Address Book window appears, highlight the person or group you want to contact and click the Send To button, or simply double-click the entry. That person's e-mail address appears in the Send To text field of the Write Mail window.

If you want to send an e-mail message to more than one person or group in the Address Book, highlight and click the Send To button for each one. America Online automatically includes each person's (or group's) screen name(s), separated by commas, and you only need to write the message once.

In AOL 7.0, your Address Book helpfully suggests e-mail addresses when you write an e-mail. Type the first letter or two into the Send To text box, and then select the full e-mail address from the drop-down menu that appears. If this feature annoys you, then use keyword **Preferences** to open the Mail Preferences dialog box and uncheck *Use my Address Book to auto-suggest e-mail addresses*.

See also "Writing an E-Mail Message," earlier in this part.

Diving into Discussion Boards

What would an online service be without discussion boards? Sharpen your cyberpencil and share your views on life, politics, hobbies — whatever makes your heart flutter. This part tells you how to find and join a discussion on the message boards.

In this part . . .

Checking for New Discussion Board Messages . . . 96

Creating a Private Discussion Area 97

Creating a Public Discussion Area 99

Discussion Boards 100

Groups@AOL 101

Inviting a Friend to Join Your Group 101

Joining a Friend's Private Discussion Group 102

Posting a Reply to a Discussion Board 102

Reading a Discussion Board Message 104

Replying to a Discussion Board via E-Mail 105

Checking for New Discussion Board Messages

Flipping through the boards and looking for new messages defines the word *tedious*. Make your life easier with the Find By drop-down list at the bottom of the discussion board window:

1. Use any Channel window (or the People Connection Communities at keyword **People Connection**) to locate the forum of your heart. Look for links like <u>Talk about Music</u> or <u>Travelers' Opinions</u>.

2. Click the online area's messages icon to enter the discussion board. You might find it when you click a button labeled (Insert Channel Name here) Talk. The discussion board window hops onto the screen, showing you a list of subject folders.

   You might see a browser window open with a title like Channel Name Community. If so, click the Message Boards button to get to the message board subject links. Click a link that you like to see the folders.

3. To sort through all the messages, highlight a folder and click the Find By drop-down list. Then select Date.

4. In the middle of this Find Since dialog box that appears, you see three radio buttons. Click the radio button next to one of the following options:

   • *New (Since last visit)* finds all the new messages since you last read the folder.

   • *In last . . . days* narrows down recently posted messages. Enter a number of days in the text box.

   • *From . . . to* finds messages within a specific date range. Enter a month and year in the appropriate text boxes. For example, if you're interested in the postings from the month of May, 2001, type **05/01** and **06/01**.

Creating a Private Discussion Area

When you find a group of people that you want to keep in touch with or you need to coordinate a set of events, think Groups@AOL. Starting a Group at Groups@AOL gives you the flexibility of a discussion board, an event list that you create as you need it, space for an online photo album so you can share the shots from that last get-together, and an area you can use to feature awesome links you find on the Web.

To start your own Group:

1. Use keyword **Groups** to open the Groups@AOL area in the browser window.

Click the Create Group button. The Before You Start: Choose a Group Type window appears, telling you the difference between a public group and a private group.

2. Click the Create Group! button under *a private group.* A window with the heading Creating a Group: Step 1 of 4 appears in the browser.

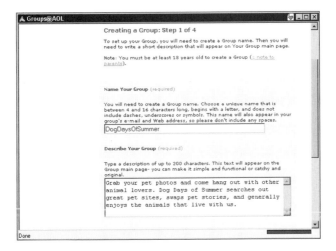

3. Think of a name for your Group that describes its purpose. Group names need to be between 4 and 16 characters long.

4. Describe your Group: its purpose, kinds of people you hope to find there, or what Group members will find when they visit.

   5. Under Select a Time Zone, check the box that signifies your agreement to follow the Groups@AOL Guidelines (read them first to ensure that you do), and click the Submit Information button.

   6. If the system doesn't like your chosen Group name, you might need to alter it a bit until Groups@AOL accepts it. Even if you need to change the "official" Group name, you can always re-type your first choice in the Choose a Title for Your Main Page text box that appears in the Creating a Group: Step 2 of 4 window.

   7. Give your main Group page a title and decide how you want the sections of your Group to appear when members visit it. Choose Family to place photos at the top of the discussion board and postings at the bottom; choose Friends to highlight the postings; choose an Activity Group to place the Events list at the top of the screen. When you've made your selections click Submit Information.

   8. In the Creating a Group: Step 3 of 4 screen, you select your Group's style. Choose Sci-fi, and each member gets to pick a robot image to represent herself when she signs up for your Group. Neutral, on the other hand, gives you classic lines with no member icons. Select your favorite and click Submit Information.

   9. The Creating a Group: Step 4 of 4 window asks you to create a Member Profile for yourself as a member of the Group and select an image (if the style you selected includes images). Click Submit Information when you're done.

Revel in the fact that you just created an online discussion area. Now you need to invite someone to join you or you'll sit there all alone. Click the First, Invite Some Members link and enter your friends', teammates', or fellow conspirators' e-mail addresses into the small text boxes in the Invite Members screen. Then write a few words that explain the purpose of your Group and click the Send button. You invitations wing their way to your friends' e-mail boxes.

To visit your Group after you create it, use keyword **My Groups**. Then click the link for the Group that you want to visit. Members can create more than one Group, and they can join Groups that other people create. You might find yourself with a whole list of Groups to select from in no time.

TIP

America Online members need to be at least 18 years old to create an AOL Group. Sorry, but that's how these things go.

See also "Groups@AOL," "Inviting a Friend to Join Your Group," and "Joining a Friend's Private Discussion Group" later in this part.

Creating a Public Discussion Area

Sometimes you want to share your favorite things with the world. Perhaps you pursue an esoteric hobby, such as reproduction vintage lace making, and you long to locate a few kindred souls. The Public Groups@AOL were created for just this purpose. Unlike the Private Groups, you don't need to be an AOL member to create a Public Group, and you can open your group to anyone on the Internet who wants to join. Or you can specify to the Groups software that you want to approve all members before they join. The choice is yours.

Creating a Public Group is much like creating a Private Group, with a few variations. Here's the drill for creating a Public Group:

1. Use keyword **Groups** to open the Groups@AOL area in the browser window.

2. Click the Create Group button. The Before You Start: Choose a Group Type window appears, telling you the difference between a public group and a private group.

3. Click the Create Group button under *a public group*. A window with the heading Creating Your Group: Step 1 of 4 appears in the browser.

4. Think of a catchy name for your Group and type it into the Name Your Group text box; then type a few sentences into the Describe Your Group text box that explain why your Group exists. Finally, in the Who Can Join This Group section, select the radio button next to *Let anyone join without my approval* or *I must approve all new members*. Click the Next Step button to continue.

5. The Creating Your Group: Step 2 of 4 screen appears. Type your name into the Your Name text boxes (First and Last) and then select your local time zone from the Select a Time Zone drop-down list. (If you want to, leave the time zone set as U.S. Eastern and any time notations that appear in your Group will jive with the AOL computers in Virginia.) Lastly, select the check box next to *I agree to the Groups@AOL Guidelines*. Click the Next Step button when you're ready to move on.

6. The next screen that appears, Creating Your Group: Step 3 of 4, guides you through placing your Group into the online Group Directory. If you agree with the AOL Group's suggestion for your group's placement, click the Next Step button to move on. For other options, click the <u>*To place your Group in a different category, click here*</u> link and browse through the options until you find a category that fits your Group. Then click the Next Step button.

7. In the Creating Your Group: Step 4 of 4 screen that appears, the Groups software asks you to create a Group e-mail address. Type your choice into the Create a Group E-mail Address text box, and click the Next Step button. The system churns for a while, and if all goes well, AOL Groups congratulates you on a job well done.

After you create a Public Group, AOL gives you no way to delete it. If you create a Public Group that you later decide you don't want to manage, your two choices are to either refuse everyone who asks to join (if you selected the *I must approve all new members* option back in Step 4), or to pass the ownership of the Group to another willing soul who wants to manage it.

Discussion Boards

Discussion (or *message*) *boards* resemble electronic bulletin boards. You wander in, read the messages that other folks have posted, and perhaps add a few messages of your own. The process is like a chat in slow motion. You get the give and take between conversers that you find in a chat room, but because time lapses between one posting and another, it might remind you a little of e-mail. Unlike e-mail, however, that goes to a particular group of people, discussion board messages are open to anyone who happens across them.

The online symbol for a discussion board is often an index card with a little red tack through it. Click anything that has this icon to go to the discussion boards for that area. (Sometimes a Messages button marks the boards. Other times the boards hang out in an area called Talk About.) Look for discussion boards on every one of America Online's channels.

Groups@AOL

Groups@AOL takes discussion boards to a whole new level. And they come in two flavors: Public and Private. You can create a Private Group that brings family members together from disparate points on the globe, or you can use Groups to manage your local soccer team, keep in touch with high school or college buddies, or to keep in touch with members of any other organization you can think of. Now you can also create Public Groups that are open to anyone on the Internet who might want to join. Terms of Service (TOS) guidelines even apply in Groups, so keep discussions clean.

After you create a Private Group that matches the desire of your heart, invite your special cadre of friends to share it with you — or create a Public Group and make new friends when you meet the people who join your Group.

See also "Creating a Private Discussion Area," "Creating a Public Discussion Area," and "Joining a Friend's Private Discussion Group" elsewhere in this part.

Inviting a Friend to Join Your Group

After you create a Groups@AOL Group, invite all your friends to join the fun! The more the merrier — although a Group with four or less people might feel really cozy, you probably won't see a lot of action in the Group unless your members are the definition of *prolific*. Of course, the Group's purpose might automatically delimit its members. A Group designed to track the kids' sports teams, for example, would include other team families.

To invite a friend to your Group:

1. First, create an online Group. ***See also*** "Creating a Private Discussion Area," and "Creating a Public Discussion Area" in this part if you need a jump-start.

2. Use keyword **My Groups** to open your main group list.

3. Click the name of the Group that you want to open to other people.

4. On the main page for your Group, look for the <u>Send an Invitation</u> link in the Owner Tools list and click it.

5. Fill in the e-mail addresses or AOL screen names of the people who you want to invite, type a message explaining what the Group does, and click the Send Invitations button.

See also "Groups@AOL," "Creating a Private Discussion Area," "Creating a Public Discussion Area," and "Joining a Friend's Private Discussion Group" elsewhere in this part.

Joining a Friend's Private Discussion Group

When one of your online buddies or neighborhood pals creates an online Group with Groups@AOL, he needs to e-mail you an invitation before you can join. When you receive the invitation in your mailbox, you have up to 60 days to respond. After that time, the invitation becomes invalid and the Group owner needs to invite you again if you still want to join.

If you receive a Groups@AOL invitation in your mailbox and you want to join, click the <u>Click Here to Join Now</u> link that's embedded in the e-mail message. The message comes from your friend's screen name@aol.com, and its subject line reads something like Please Join This Group!

If you decide you want to pass on this Group opportunity, close the e-mail and do nothing. The invitation expires on its own. (Of course, a reply message to the sender thanking her for the invitation is always in good taste, even if you decide not to join.)

Posting a Reply to a Discussion Board

Lively discussion requires two-way conversation. On the America Online discussion boards, posting a reply to someone's comment enables you to add your opinions to the topic at hand. You can either reply publicly to the board itself or you can reply privately via e-mail.

When you reply to the board itself, your input is public. Anyone can browse the boards and see what you've written. To reply to the discussion boards, follow these steps:

1. Find a message that you want to discuss and click the Reply button. Keep in mind that a good reply sticks to the discussion at hand.

2. The Reply window opens, and the subject line is already entered. In most cases, leave the subject line as it appears so that others can follow the discussion.

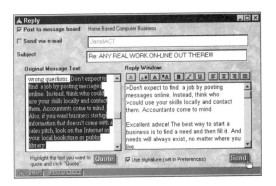

3. Enter your response in the Reply Window box. Use the formatting buttons along the top edge of the text box to jazz up your post.

4. To include some or all of the previous poster's message in your reply, use the Original Message Text box and highlight the words, sentences, or phrases that you want to include. Then click the Quote button. The highlighted text jumps into the Reply Window, complete with a message board quote mark.

5. Either sign your name or your America Online screen name at the bottom of the message, or select the *Use signature* check box at the bottom of the message box. This action places a signature line at the end of your message posts (if you created one).

6. Select the *Send via e-mail* check box to send your post to the author of the original message, select the *Post to message board* check box to add your thoughts to the message thread, or check, them both.

7. Click the Send button and the message disappears to fulfill your commands.

Click the Preferences button at the bottom of any of the colorful message board windows to set your Message Board Preferences. These preferences let you sort messages, show messages posted within so many days, or add a special signature to your message board posts. If you run a business, engage in a particular hobby, or center your life around your pets, you might want to create signature lines such as *John Doe, Owner, Pets Unlimited; JSKaufeld, Lacemaker;* or *Bill, My Cat, Is My Life.* Be creative — but remember, even signature lines need to fall within Terms of Service guidelines.

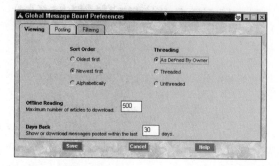

Reading a Discussion Board Message

After you locate a discussion board that follows a topic that interests you, the next task is to read what others have to say. To find out what others members think about a topic, read the messages posted in a discussion board. You read a message by following these steps:

1. Open the online area and look for the discussion board icon. You might see a square icon that looks like a note fastened with a pin, or you might find a button cleverly labeled Messages or Boards.

   Some of the newly redesigned areas online feature a <u>Message Boards</u> link (or button) or a series of tabs marked Chat, Boards, Home Pages, and Features. Click the link or the tab to begin your journey towards the discussion boards.

2. Double-click the icon or click the button to open the Messages window.

3. Highlight a topic in the Topics list and click the List All button.

4. Highlight a Subject and click the Read Post button. A message window opens and shows the first message.

5. To read all the postings under that subject, click the Next Post button when you want to move forward. To jump to the next subject, click the Subject->> button. When any arrow turns gray, you've reached the end of the messages in that direction.

After you visit a discussion board for the first time, on your next visit you can click the List Unread button rather than the List All button to see the new topics and pick up where you left off.

See also "Posting a Reply to a Discussion Board" and "Checking for New Discussion Board Messages" elsewhere in this part.

Replying to a Discussion Board via E-Mail

Replying to a discussion post via e-mail enables you to voice your opinions privately to the original poster. These messages never reach the discussion boards. Instead, they go directly to the America Online member's mailbox. To post a reply, follow these steps:

1. Click the Reply button to open the Post A Reply message box.

2. Highlight in the Original Message Text box any material that you want to include from the previous post. Then click the Quote button.

3. Write your response in the Reply Window text box.

4. Sign your name.

5. Select the *Send via e-mail* check box.

6. Deselect (uncheck) the *Post to message board* check box.

7. Click the Send button.

See also Part V for more on the ins and outs of electronic mail (e-mail).

Saving and Sharing Pictures Online

Forget taking your photo scrapbook to the next family get-together — with You've Got Pictures, you can create online picture albums to feature your favorite shots and swap with others. Create a photo album and send it to family members before the big day so you can spend the afternoon talking about the shots instead of peering over them.

In this part ...

Changing Your Online Album. 108
Creating Albums. 109
Developing You've Got Pictures 112
Receiving Buddy Albums. 113
Saving Your Pictures Online 115
Sharing the Buddy Albums You Create. 115
Using You've Got Pictures with Digital Photos . . . 117
You've Got Pictures 119

Changing Your Online Album

After you create an online photo album, it's ready to share with friends and family. If you want to tweak a picture here or a caption there before you send your masterpiece over the Net, you can edit any of your online albums. Much like everything else in the You've Got Pictures area, nothing is set in stone — if you decide you want to change something, you can.

To edit an online album:

1. Open the You've Got Pictures area by clicking the You've Got Pictures icon in the Welcome window or using keyword **Pictures**.

2. Click the Go To My Pictures button in the AOL You've Got Pictures window to see the list of albums you created. The My Rolls & Albums tab should be active.

3. Click the album title that awaits a special editing touch. The album appears in the You've Got Pictures browser window.

4. Click the Edit Album button. The album reappears in the Edit My Album window with a set of editing buttons along the bottom of the window.

5. Check any photo's box to select it, and then change it as you like. In the Edit Album window, you can:

• Re-caption photos by selecting a picture and clicking the Captions button.

- Change the album title or description with the Title button.
- Change the album's background color with the Layout button.
- Also use the Layout button to alter the picture layout.
- Add or remove pictures from the album.

6. When everything looks perfect, click Save to make your changes real. If you have second thoughts, clicking the Cancel button deletes all your changes.

See also "Creating Albums" later in this part.

Creating Albums

After you hear the cheery "You've Got Pictures" welcome when you sign on to America Online, you can make your own online picture albums and then share them with others. Pictures appear in your You've Got Pictures area in three ways:

✔ You have pictures developed, and your developer adds the new photos to your You've Got Pictures account.

✔ You upload pictures from your hard drive that you took with your digital camera (*see also* "Using You've Got Pictures with Digital Photos" later in this part).

✔ A friend sends you a Buddy Album that he or she created using his or her own pictures.

Creating albums from your pictures

After you get new pictures developed and sent to your You've Got Pictures account, you can create an album. You can also create albums from digital pictures you've saved on your hard drive. To create an album from your pictures, follow these steps:

1. Use keyword **Pictures** to open the You've Got Pictures window.

2. Click the Go To My Pictures button in the You've Got Pictures window to open your online photo area.

3. Click the My Rolls & Albums tab to open your list of photo collections if it's not already active when the browser window opens.

4. Click the Your Saved Pictures link to view the pictures you've saved online.

5. Click to select the pictures that you want to display in your album.

6. Click the Create New Album button. The Create New Album window appears, showing the photos that you selected.

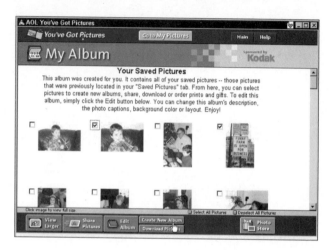

7. Customize your album with the Create New Album options.

• **Add Pictures:** Place additional pictures into your album. Select from other albums you've created, Buddy Albums that you receive, or other saved pictures.

• **Delete:** Take pictures out of the album. Click to select the picture and then click the Remove Pictures button.

• **Title:** Give the album a more captivating name than *Your Saved Pictures* and create a more captivating description than *This album was created for you,* the default names America Online uses.

• **Captions:** Give your picture a name or description. .

• **Layout:** Decide whether you want your pictures to appear one, two, or four to a row, and click accordingly. Also use this button to select a background color for your album.

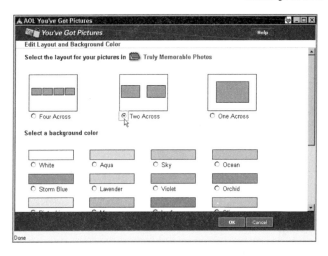

8. When you've spiffed up your album, click Save to make your changes real.

Creating albums from Buddy Albums you receive

Friends and family may create Buddy Albums and send them to you. To create an album from a Buddy Album you have received, follow these steps:

1. An e-mail message entitled `screen name has sent you the Buddy Album` and the album name appears in your Online Mailbox to tell you someone has sent you a Buddy Album.

2. Use keyword **Pictures** to retrieve your Buddy Album. If you've already viewed the Buddy Album, look for it under the Buddy Albums tab. If you haven't seen the album yet, look for it under the New Pictures tab.

3. Select the pictures that you want to include in your own album by checking each photo's box.

4. Click the Create New Album button. The photos appear in a new Edit My Album window.

5. All the options appear as described in Step 7 of the preceding numbered list. Customize your album and then click Save to make your changes permanent.

6. Now the newly created album appears in place under the My Rolls & Albums tab, and you can send the album to your online friends.

See also "Developing You've Got Pictures," "Sharing the Buddy Albums You Create," and "Receiving Buddy Albums" later in this part.

Developing You've Got Pictures

AOL's You've Got Pictures service places your newly developed photos online so that you can create online photo albums to share. You can also download individual pictures onto your hard drive to use in newsletters or print out for friends.

To use You've Got Pictures, take your pictures to an authorized You've Got Pictures photo developer. After looking at the list of developers available in my neighborhood, I imagine that your local photo developer probably participates in this program.

Here's how to find out which developers participate in your area:

1. Use keyword **Pictures** to open the You've Got Pictures window in your browser.

2. Click the <u>Find a Local Photo Developer</u> link. The Find Your Local Photo Developer window opens.

3. Enter your zip code into the text box and then click the Find Now button. The system offers a list of developers, along with addresses and phone numbers.

When you take your film for processing, check the AOL You've Got Pictures box on the film envelope and fill in your e-mail address (screen name @aol.com). That way, when the film is ready, you get an e-mail notification. If you hear the familiar "You've Got Pictures" announcement when you sign on to AOL, you know that the pictures have been scanned and are ready for viewing online.

Keyword **Pictures** takes you to the You've Got Pictures area. Click the Go To My Pictures button to open your online pictures section and automatically open the New Rolls section.

Remember: Using the You've Got Pictures service costs an extra $4.95 per roll at the developer.

After your pictures are online, you can do the following:

- ✔ Look at them by clicking the New Pictures tab in the You've Got Pictures browser window.

- ✔ Save the pictures to your online storage area by clicking the roll's link to view the pictures. The pictures then take their place in your growing Your Saved Pictures album under the My Rolls & Albums tab.

- ✔ Give the film roll a new name. Something a little more intuitive than *MYKAUF231359* would be nice. Use a descriptive name like *Summer Vacation 2000.*

- ✔ Create and edit your own online albums from your saved pictures. Click the My Rolls & Albums tab to get started.

- ✔ Share your newly created albums with friends and family. Click the My Rolls & Albums tab, select an album, and then click the Share Pictures button to begin.

 TIP

You have 15 days to view the pictures in your new roll or a friend's Buddy Album before they're deleted from the service. To keep the roll from expiring, either save the roll online by viewing the pictures or download the pictures into your computer.

See also "Creating Albums," "Sharing the Buddy Albums You Create," and "Receiving Buddy Albums" elsewhere in this part.

Receiving Buddy Albums

AOL calls albums that members share with each other Buddy Albums. When someone sends you a Buddy Album through You've Got Pictures, you're greeted by a "You've Got Pictures" announcement when you sign on.

You also receive an e-mail telling you who sent you the Buddy Album. The e-mail comes from screen name AOL BuddyPics, and when you open it, the message shows you the first picture from the album so you know what you're in for. (With Great Aunt Gertrude e-mailing you her favorite snapshots, that might be a good thing.)

To receive the Buddy Album, follow these steps:

1. Click the You've Got Pictures button in the Welcome window (or use keyword **Pictures**) to open You've Got Pictures in the Web browser.

2. Click the New Pictures tab if it isn't already active.

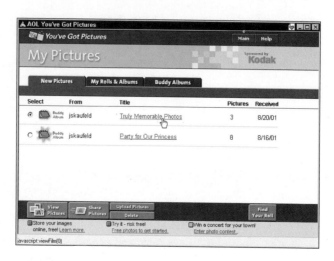

3. Select the radio button next to the title of the new Buddy Album if your Buddy Album page contains more than one. Your latest Buddy Album should appear at the top of the list already selected, unless you receive several albums a day.

4. Click the album title to open it.

5. The Buddy Album appears onscreen, complete with a link that allows you to <u>Send a message back to</u> the person who sent you the album in the first place.

You can also use the e-mail that you receive from AOL BuddyPics to see your album. Open the e-mail and click the <u>Click here to view the entire album of pictures</u> link. (The link takes you to `http://aolsvc.pictures.aol.com/`, the You've Got Pictures Web site.) When the You've Got Pictures browser window opens with the New Pictures tab active, you can click the <u>Buddy Album</u> link to view the pictures that your friend sent you.

See also "Creating Albums," "Developing You've Got Pictures," and "Sharing the Buddy Albums You Create," elsewhere in this part.

Saving Your Pictures Online

When the cheery "You've Got Pictures" notification greets you when you sign online, you know that you have received new pictures to view and save.

Saving an entire roll of film

Because new pictures expire 15 days after they appear online, you need to save them to your online storage area if you want to keep them.

To save an entire roll of film:

1. Click the You've Got Pictures button in the Welcome window. Your private You've Got Pictures area opens, showing an active New Pictures tab.

2. If you have more than one new roll waiting for you, select the radio button next to the roll that you want to choose.

3. Click the roll's linked title to view and save the entire roll of pictures.

Saving new pictures one by one

If you don't remember what's on that particular roll of film and you want to take a peek before you save the pictures, you can save them one by one. To view and then save your online pictures:

1. Click the You've Got Pictures button in the Welcome screen. Your private You've Got Pictures area opens, displaying the New Pictures tab and its contents.

2. Select the roll that you want to see from the rolls listed in the New Pictures tab.

3. Click the View Pictures button. After a bit of a wait, each picture loads into your browser window.

4. Check the box next to any picture you want to save from the roll, and then click the Save button. You've Got Pictures then saves the individual shots instead of the entire roll — a handy option if you only want specific shots saved online.

Sharing the Buddy Albums You Create

Your album is freshly created, you feel like a photo pro, and you're ready to share your pictures with buddies far and wide. Sharing Buddy Albums is really easy — America Online and You've Got

Pictures do all the hard work. You supply the e-mail address or addresses of the people you want to receive the albums, and AOL packages them up and ships them off along with an e-mail to that person telling them that you sent them a Buddy Album. Pretty cool, eh?

To send someone a Buddy Album:

1. Click the You've Got Pictures icon in the Welcome window to go to the You've Got Pictures area.

2. Click the Go To My Pictures button to open your saved online photos.

3. If the My Rolls & Albums tab isn't already active, click it.

4. Click the radio button next to the album title that you want to share.

5. Click the Share Pictures button. If this is the first time that you create a Buddy Album, the You've Got Pictures Agreement hops to the screen, with a very general explanation of copyright law. Read the information so you know what is and isn't kosher, and then click the Accept button to make the agreement go away.

6. The Share Pictures screen appears in the browser window. If you want to change the name of your album when you send it, type in the new name in the *Sending pictures as an album named* text box.

7. Type the recipient's screen name or Internet e-mail address into the Send To text box. If you've recently shared an album with anyone, use the Add Names from Share List button to select additional people to receive your album.

8. Use the E-Mail Message box to include additional information about your album, a greeting to the people receiving it, or anything else appropriate to the occasion.

9. When you're happy with the list, click the Send button. You've Got Pictures explains that it sent your album to your list of buddies.

10. Click OK.

See also "Creating Albums" earlier in this part.

Using You've Got Pictures with Digital Photos

You've Got Pictures gives digital camera owners an easy way to create online photo albums and share photos via e-mail. To use You've Got Pictures with digital photos, upload the photos stored on your hard drive into the You've Got Pictures storage area. Here's how:

1. Save your digital photos to your hard drive if they aren't there already.

2. Use keyword **Pictures** to go to the You've Got Pictures area.

3. Click the Upload Pictures button in the You've Got Pictures window. The Upload My Album window appears.

4. Click the button next to a new album to create a unique area for your uploaded pictures. Otherwise AOL drops the photos into one of your already created albums, a most unhandy option unless you're a lot more organized than I am.

   If you like, you can even give your new uploaded pictures a name before you begin the process; I generally use the generic `Pictures Uploaded on date` so that I know these photos came from my hard drive.

5. Select your uploading option: You can upload one picture at a time or multiple pictures at a time. The choice is yours.

   • To upload a single picture, click the Upload Single Picture button and continue with Step 6 below.

   • To upload several pictures at one time, click Upload Multiple Pictures. This option requires an extra download, which begins when you click Install in the screen that appears.

   • After you install the Upload Multiple Pictures option, You've Got Pictures automatically assumes that this is the course you want to take every time that you upload photos to your private You've Got Pictures area. If you ever want to upload one picture at a time, click the <u>Single-Picture Upload</u> tool link in the Upload Multiple Pictures browser window to do the single-picture upload thing.

6. Locate the file on your hard drive and click the Open button. The filename appears in the text box next to the Browse button.

   To upload several pictures at a time, locate the folder on your hard drive and then select the pictures you want to upload. Continue with Step 8.

7. To double-check what you're uploading, click the Preview Picture button. A small version of the photo appears under to the Preview Picture button.

8. Click Upload Picture, and the file uploads to your My Rolls &
Albums area.

9. The picture appears in the browser when it's uploaded; click
the Go to My Pictures button to return to the main You've Got
Pictures area or click the Upload More button to repeat the
process with another file.

Look for your new uploaded album at the top of the list in the
My Rolls & Albums tab.

You need to store digital photos in JPG, JPEG, GIF, or BMP formats
for You've Got Pictures to accept them.

You've Got Pictures

You've Got Pictures is an America Online feature that lets you keep
digital copies of developed photos online. If you take your film to a
local photo developer that uses the You've Got Pictures service,
you get your prints — and an electronic version of the roll appears
in your private You've Got Pictures area of America Online.

You've Got Pictures enables you to save pictures, create photo
albums to share with friends and family via e-mail, and even purchase gifts from Kodak that feature your photos. Use keyword
Pictures to get started.

See also "Creating Albums," "Developing You've Got Pictures,"
"Receiving Buddy Albums," and "Saving Your Pictures Online"
earlier in this part.

Downloading, Logging, Printing, and Saving

Mining for informational nuggets and inexpensive new software makes the online world a never-ending adventure. Of course, searching is only the first step; after that comes capturing. This part explores your tools for nabbing online information and tucking it away on your hard drive or saving a copy on paper.

In this part ...

Checking File Descriptions 122

Choosing Where to Store Files to Download 122

Downloading Files from E-Mail Messages 122

Downloading Files Later
    (The Download Manager) 123

Downloading Files Right Now 124

Finding Files to Download 126

Logging Chats, IMs, and Sessions 126

Printing 128

Saving Text from a Window 128

Seeing Which Files You've Already Downloaded . . 129

Uploading Files 129

ZIP Files 131

Checking File Descriptions

To check a description of a file waiting to be downloaded, double-click the file's entry in the Download Manager list. The description window pops up with all the information available about that particular file.

Remember: This trick won't work if you're not signed on to America Online.

See also "Downloading Files Later (The Download Manager)" in this part.

Choosing Where to Store Files to Download

To tell the Download Manager where to store the files it downloads to your hard drive, open the Download Manager window (keyword **Download Manager**) and then click the Select Destination button. In the Select path dialog box, navigate the folders to click your way to the right path. If you decide not to change the storage location, look for all your files in your Download folder.

Don't worry if the word path is in the File name area of the dialog box — that's normal, if somewhat odd, behavior.

See also "Downloading Files Later (The Download Manager)" later in this part.

Downloading Files from E-Mail Messages

Thanks to the technical wonders of America Online, downloading the files you receive through e-mail is easy:

1. Double-click the message to open it.

2. Click the Download button at the bottom of the message and select one of the two options that appear — Download Now or Download Later.

- **Download Now:** Opens the Download Manager dialog box so that you can select a destination and then click Save.

- **Download Later:** Places the file in the Download Manager. When you're ready to download, choose File⇨Download Manager to open the Download Manager window. If necessary, click the Select Destination button to change where the file will be placed on your hard drive. Finally, click Download.

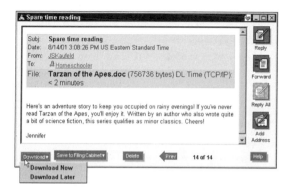

 To be safe in these times of unmuzzled hackers on the Internet, never download *any* file from *anyone* you don't know. The 7.0 version of the software allows you to send multiple attachments in e-mail, but only the first attachment's name shows in the recipient's mail message. Thus, the first attachment might be a text file, but a subsequent attachment could be an executable virus. Better to be safe and apologize later than experience the time and trouble of recovering from a hacker's twisted joke.

See also "Downloading Files Later (The Download Manager)" later in this part.

Downloading Files Later (The Download Manager)

AOL's Download Manager tracks files that you mark with the Download Later button, and it remembers the files that you downloaded in the past. It's pretty bright — it even knows how to unpack ZIP files.

To open the Download Manager, choose Files⇨Download Manager. The Download Manager window lists all files that are waiting to be downloaded. When you click Download Later while looking at a file, the Download Manager stores that file's information in this window.

Remember: If you change your mind and want to remove files from the list before downloading the rest, click the filename that you want to remove and then click the Remove Item button. It's outta there.

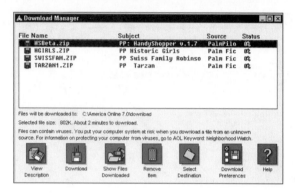

Turn to *America Online 7.0 For Dummies,* by John Kaufeld (Hungry Minds, Inc.) for even more downloading tips and tricks.

Downloading Files Right Now

A world of stuff awaits you in the America Online file libraries. Programs, information, graphics, and more — they're all just a download away. Just follow these steps:

1. In your favorite online area, find the file library (almost every area has one). Look for a button labeled *Software, Files, Cool Stuff, Downloads,* or something like that. A window appears, listing different software categories.

If you're in a particularly small online area, you may go directly to a list of available files. In that case, skip to Step 3.

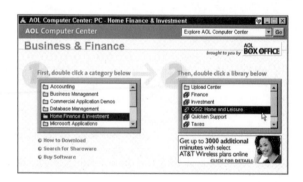

2. Pick a category that looks interesting and double-click it. A list of available files pops onto the screen.

If you're in a particularly large online area, this window may contain another list of categories, like those in Step 1. In that case, repeat this step (Step 2) until you get to a file list.

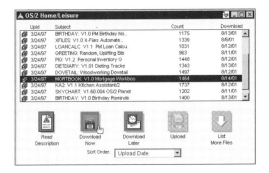

3. Scroll through the list until you find a file that looks interesting. To organize files by popularity or by subject, click the arrow next to the Sort Order box at the bottom of the file list window. Select your preferred sorting method there (Upload Date, Subject, Download Count, or Download Date) and watch the items fall into line.

4. At this point, you can look at the file's description, download it, or mark it for downloading later.

  • **To see a description of the file:** Double-click the file's entry in the list. A window that tells you everything you ever wanted to know about the file hops onto the screen.

  • **To download the file right now:** Click the Download Now button. When the Download Manager window pops up, select a destination for the file (and change the filename, if you like). When you're ready to go, click Save or press Enter. The file begins to make its way to your computer.

  • **To download the file later:** Click the Download Later button. America Online notes the filename and location in the Download Manager and presents a dialog box onscreen telling you that the file was successfully added to your download list.

Remember: If you choose Download Later, remember to start the Download Manager sometime (choose File⇨Download Manager) and finish transferring the file to your computer.

If you forget to start the Download Manager later to download files, don't worry. When you sign off, the software politely shows you a dialog box that asks whether you want to download the files that you marked earlier.

See also "Downloading Files Later (The Download Manager)" earlier in this part.

Finding Files to Download

America Online offers a marvelously extensive software library with files for Macintosh, Windows, and other operating systems and computers. Locate them in two ways:

- ✔ **To browse through file lists:** Use keyword **Download Center** to open the main PC Download Center screen. Remember that most online areas have their own software libraries as well.

- ✔ **To search the online libraries:** Use keyword **Download Center**, and then click the Shareware button under Search for Software. The main Software Search window covers primarily Windows programs.

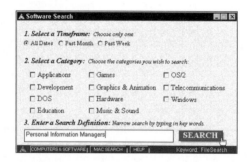

See also "Downloading Files Right Now" and "Downloading Files Later (The Download Manager)" earlier in this part.

Logging Chats, IMs, and Sessions

Following everything that's going on in a chat room — or everything that you're doing online, for that matter — can be tough, particularly if you're distracted by a constant stream of Instant Messages or a dog with a small bladder. To combat this problem, America Online includes a recording feature called Logs. Logs store every word or piece of text that appears on your screen.

If you're a newshound, the Session Logs feature can save you a great deal of time and effort. Session Logs record all the text windows you open while you're on America Online. This feature includes news stories, stock portfolio information, file descriptions — almost all the informational text that America Online sends to you. You can even capture Instant Messages with Session Logs! On the other hand, use the Chat Logs feature to take minutes at online club meetings, record a special online presentation, or just track who said what.

Use the logging feature to track:

- ✔ Entire online sessions
- ✔ Chats you attend
- ✔ Instant Messages you receive and send

Remember: You need to open a new Log each time you sign onto the system if you want to track sessions, chats, or IMs.

Here's how to use the logging feature:

1. Choose File⇨Log Manager. The Logging dialog box appears.

2. Click the Open Log button.

   To log a chat, you click the Open Log button in the Chat Log area of the window. The Open Log dialog box appears, displaying the name of the chat room as the filename.

   To log an entire session, click the Open Log button in the Session Log area of the window. The Open Log dialog box appears, displaying the word *session* as the filename.

3. Press Enter or click Save. The log is on and ready to record.

   To log Instant Messages, first open a Session Log in Steps 2 and 3, and then check the *Log Instant Message conversations* check box.

4. To close the log when you finish, choose File⇨Log Manager; then click the Close Log button.

Remember: You can't view the log file until you close it, and you need to be in a chat room before the Chat Log buttons become active. When you close the log, it saves to your system. Look for it in the Download folder, or wherever you told AOL to place files you download to your computer.

Logs are plain text files, so you can use any word processor or text editor to open them.

Printing

When you want a permanent copy of something cool you find online, try printing it. Within America Online, you can print text windows and many online graphics, plus most Web pages. You can't print menu lists, though. To print something:

1. Open the window that you want to print.

2. Choose Print⇨Print. The Print dialog box appears.

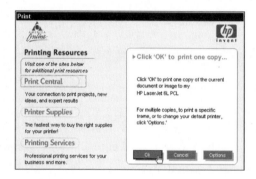

3. Make sure that your printer is online; then press Enter or click OK to print.

Unless you're in a text-only window, such as a message board posting, you may receive a surprise when you try to print from the screen. Sometimes printing a document gives you the graphic; other times, you receive just the text. Often (especially if the top of the window reads something like `Printing Graphic 1 of 2`), you get both.

Saving Text from a Window

If a news story, information window, e-mail message, or Web site sparks your interest, save a copy of the item on your computer. Here's how:

1. Browse through the system until you find some text that looks interesting enough to keep.

2. Choose File⇨Save. The Save As dialog box pops up.

3. Unless you specify somewhere else, America Online saves the file to the AOL Download folder on your hard drive. Type a filename for the text file you're creating in the *File name* text box.

4. When you finish, press Enter or click Save. America Online creates a file for the text and saves it on your computer where you specified.

To save a link to the story or online item instead of saving the entire thing to your hard drive, use the Favorite Places feature. **See also** Part II for more about Favorite Places.

Seeing Which Files You've Already Downloaded

From the Download Manager, you can look at a list of files you've already downloaded. Just click the Show Files Downloaded button. The Files You've Downloaded window appears. By default, it shows your last 100 downloads.

If you want America Online to remember more (or fewer) than 100 files, click the Download Preferences button on the Download Manager window and change the number entered in the *Retain information about my last X downloads* option, where X is the number of downloads.

Uploading Files

Submitting a file to other America Online members gives you a good feeling, like you're contributing to the community. Whenever you can, offer something to the online community by uploading your favorite shareware programs or artwork.

Remember that you can only upload freeware or shareware programs, text files that you wrote, or artwork that you created. You can't upload commercial programs. (In fact, America Online will probably cancel your account if you do because uploading commercial programs violates Federal copyright law.)

To submit a file to America Online, just follow these steps:

1. Use a keyword or menu selection to get into an online area that covers the subject of your file. You usually find files and uploading options in the various channel communities, so use keyword **Communities** to locate your favorite channel chatter.

2. Look for a menu entry labeled Library, File Library, or something similar (unfortunately, I can't be more specific — the exact name is up to the folks who run the area) and double-click it to view the area's Library window.

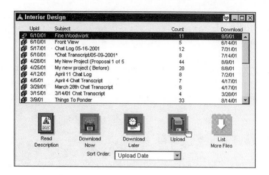

3. Click the Upload button on the File Library window. The Upload dialog box appears.

If you don't see an Upload button, AOL is probably trying to tell you that this particular area doesn't accept files from members. Not every library takes uploads. If you aren't sure whether that particular library accepts uploads, send an e-mail message to the forum leader and ask for information and guidelines for posting.

4. Fill out the informational entries in the Upload File window. Pay particular attention to the Needs and Description sections. People who want to download your file rely on you for this information.

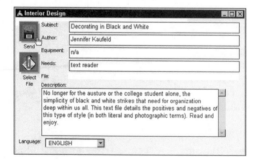

5. Click the Select File button. The Attach File dialog box pops up.

6. Find your file among the teeming multitudes in the dialog box list. To include the file in your upload, double-click its entry. The Upload File dialog box shows the name of the file that's destined for America Online.

7. When all looks ready to go, click the Send button to upload your file.

If you want to upload a computer-related or electronic text file, keyword **Upload** sends you directly to the AOL Computer Center uploading section. Select the appropriate file library from the list and go from there.

ZIP Files

In the world of Windows and DOS, ZIP files rule as the undisputed leaders of file compression. Although the America Online Version 7.0 software understands ZIP files, having your own unzipping software handy is still a good idea.

In a Windows environment, the popular choice is the WinZip program (it's so popular that keyword **WinZip** leads to the AOL Computer Center's How to Download window). To download a copy, use keyword **WinZip** and click the Handling MIME and ZIP Files link.

Exploring the
Internet

When the Internet quietly started back in the mid '60s, few people guessed that it would turn into the worldwide power that it is today. What began as a small military experiment grew slowly through the '70s, matured in the '80s, and absolutely exploded in the '90s.

Today, this global network of networks offers an incredible array of information with mailing lists, newsgroups, file transfer protocol (FTP) sites, and the World Wide Web. Best of all, each one of these information services is available through America Online.

In this part . . .

E-Mail 134
File Transfer Protocol (FTP) 134
Mailing Lists 138
Newsgroups 139
Search Systems on the Net 147
Winsock Applications and AOL 147
World Wide Web Adventures 148

E-Mail

Electronic mail was the Internet's first application — this is where it all started. America Online continues the tradition with an Internet mail gateway, giving you the ability to send mail to both America Online members *and* nonmembers who have Internet mail addresses.

See also "Mailing Lists" later in this part, and check out Part V for a close inspection of the hows, whys, and how-tos of electronic mail and the Internet.

File Transfer Protocol (FTP)

The Internet, being the odd place that it is, uses its own special system for downloading files. *FTP,* short for File Transfer Protocol, is the Internet's file transfer magician. FTP is sometimes called *Anonymous FTP* because most of the computers that offer files through FTP don't ask you for a special password. Because the computers are open to everyone, the service is deemed *anonymous.*

To get into the FTP area, use keyword **FTP**. From the FTP – File Transfer Protocol window that appears, you can check out some general FTP information, search for FTP sites, or set up a connection to a particular site.

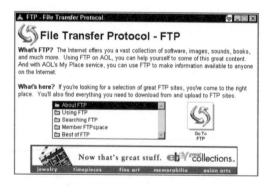

Don't download files through FTP unless you have a virus-checking program installed and running on your computer. Carefully virus-check *absolutely every file* you get through FTP — don't trust *anything.* (For more information about viruses, the havoc they can wreak, and what to do about them, visit the online Anti-Virus Center at keyword **Virus**.)

Downloading files from FTP sites

Copying a file from an FTP site isn't too hard, but the process is a little more complicated than downloading a file from America Online.

1. From the FTP window, click the Go to FTP button. The Anonymous FTP window appears.

2. Pick an FTP site from the list or use the address of another site.

 • **To choose a site from the list in the Anonymous FTP window:** Scroll through the list until you find the site that you want; then double-click its entry.

 • **To enter your own special address:** Click the Other Site button. In the Other Site dialog box that opens, type your address in the Site Address text box and then click the Connect button.

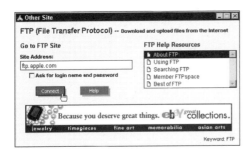

Either way that you choose an FTP site, America Online responds after a moment, either to report that you made the connection or that something didn't work right. If you success-fully connect to the FTP site, a list window shows all the files available in the FTP computer's current directory. If the con-nection doesn't work, America Online suggests that you check your spelling and try again.

If you read something about *mirror access* in the FTP window, that's okay. That message means that you connected to a copy (or *mirror*) of the FTP site, created by America Online to give you faster access to the same information. Pretty cool, eh?

3. Browse by double-clicking entries on the list. (Enjoy yourself — this is the fun part.)

4. When an entry piques your interest, click it. If the Download Now button comes to life, that entry is available for downloading. If not, then the file isn't available. After you click Download Now,

America Online briefly puts up a Retrieving Data dialog box. Behind the scenes, the AOL computers are copying the file at very high speed from wherever it happens to be on the Internet. When the AOL computers finish receiving the file, the Download Manager window appears on-screen, asking what you want to call the file on your computer.

5. Type a name for the file into the Filename text box of the Download Manager window and then press Enter. The download starts immediately.

6. When the file finishes downloading, America Online beeps and tosses up a simple report announcing that the file arrived safely.

7. To download more files, repeat Steps 4–6. After you finish, close the FTP window by clicking the X in the upper-right corner.

Closing the FTP window when you finish downloading is very important. America Online keeps a connection open to the FTP site until you close the site's window. Because many sites limit the number of people who can download things at once, other people on the Net may not be able to access the site until you leave by closing the FTP window.

Uploading to FTP sites

Some (but not all) FTP sites accept file uploads from Internet users. If you have software to share, consider uploading to an FTP site.

Only upload files that you wrote or shareware programs — don't even *think* about uploading a copy of your favorite commercial program or game. (I don't want you to break the copyright laws! Keyword **Copyright** tells you more about what is and isn't legal.) To upload files to an FTP site, follow these steps:

1. In the FTP window (keyword **FTP**), click the Go to FTP button, and the FTP window opens.

2. To connect to the site you want, click the Other Site button. The Other Site window opens; type your address in the Site Address text box. When you're finished, press Enter or click the Connect button. If the connection works, you're in; if it doesn't, check the spelling and try again. The correct name opens the FTP site's window.

3. In the FTP site's window, click the Upload button. A filename dialog box appears.

   If the Upload button doesn't appear on your screen, then you can't upload files to this FTP site. Sorry, but that's how it goes.

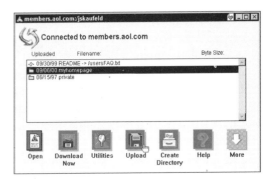

4. Type the name of the file *as you want it to appear on the FTP server.* You're not telling America Online where to find the file on your computer yet. Instead, the software wants to know what to call the copy that you're uploading to the FTP computer.

5. If you're uploading a plain text file, select the ASCII radio button. If the file is anything other than plain text, select the Binary radio button.

6. Double-check your entries and then click the Continue button. The Upload File dialog box appears.

7. Click the Select File button. The Attach File dialog box pops up.

8. Scroll through the dialog box until you find the file to send; then double-click it. The file's name and path appear in the File dialog box.

9. Click the Send button to start the transfer. A File Transfer dialog box updates you on the file transfer status. An annoying little dialog box tells you that the transfer is complete; click OK to make it go away.

10. To send more files, repeat Steps 3 through 9. After you finish sending files, close the FTP window.

If you want to upload files to your private Web space on AOL, use keyword **My FTP Space** and then click the See My FTP Space button. You go directly to a window labeled members.aol.com/ screen name. Open the Private folder and begin at Step 3 of the previous steps.

See also "World Wide Web Adventures" later in this part.

Using a particular FTP site

Getting into a specific site is easy with the America Online FTP system. Here's how:

1. From the FTP window, click the Go To FTP button.

2. In the Anonymous FTP window, click the Other Site button. The Other Site dialog box appears.

3. Type the address of the FTP site that you want into the text box; then either press Enter or click the Connect button.

The addresses usually start with FTP, such as `ftp.apple.com` and `ftp.microsoft.com`. If the address you have starts with `www`, then the address is for a World Wide Web site.

See also "World Wide Web Adventures" later in this part.

Mailing Lists

Internet mailing lists are discussion groups that meet in your e-mail box. They carry on the same sort of debates as network newsgroups — in fact, some newsgroups and mailing lists share postings with each other.

Mailing lists are easy to work with and (usually) free. The downside is often the sheer number of messages that they steer into your mailbox. Keep in mind the following guidelines:

✔ Join lists one by one — not several at one time. Get a feel for how much traffic a new list carries before joining another.

✔ Don't join a list unless you plan to stay for a while. Joining a list and immediately unsubscribing is very rude.

Finding a good mailing list often resembles a cloak-and-dagger mission. Keep your eyes open while you cruise America Online — sometimes you stumble across a mailing list mentioned in a discussion board or chat room. Perhaps an e-mail buddy who shares your interests gives you a mailing list address. If all else fails, search the list at PAML, the Publicly Accessible Mailing Lists compilation (`paml.net`). PAML includes lists by subject, along with all the information you need to join (or leave).

Also take a look at eGroups, which hosts mailing lists that cover a myriad of topics. View the list at `groups.yahoo.com` at the Yahoo! Groups site.

After you join a list, your mailbox starts filling up with messages from list members. The number of messages varies, depending on the list. Read your mail regularly and keep up with the messages; otherwise, the incoming messages may fill your mailbox to overflowing.

Remember: If you join a list, don't be surprised when you start getting junk e-mail. Unethical marketing companies copy e-mail addresses from mailing-list databases and use those addresses for unsolicited mailings. This practice is an unfortunate and unintended side effect of subscribing.

Newsgroups

Shortly after the Internet started, the researchers who were using it created an electronic bulletin board for online discussions. This bulletin board evolved into the Internet *newsgroups,* a collection of several thousand rollicking conversations covering computers, hard science, industrial music, and almost everything in between. America Online offers a very complete collection of the world's newsgroups.

The Terms of Service (TOS) rules, which give America Online its family orientation, *don't* extend into the Internet newsgroups. Free, uncensored speech is the rule, not the exception. If frank (and sometimes downright rude) language offends your sensibilities, then stay out of the newsgroups. I'm not trying to scare you; I just want you to know what you're getting into.

Newsgroups are organized in hierarchies by topic. Eight main hierarchies (plus hundreds of smaller, secondary ones) are available.

Newsgroup	*Hierarchy*	*Content*
alt	Alternative	Anything from music to religion to plastic utensil collecting — this is the wildest place on the Internet
comp	Computers	Anything and everything about computers and software
misc	Miscellaneous	Newsgroups that don't fit anywhere else land here
news	News	News about the Internet itself, not current events
rec	Recreation	Includes sport, game, and hobby newsgroups for all ages and interests
sci	Science	Big-time scientific discussions among researchers all over the world
soc	Sociology	Discussions among sociologists covering whatever it is they talk about
talk	Talk	Talk, talk, and more talk

To get into the Newsgroups window, use keyword **Newsgroups** or choose Services⇨Internet from the toolbar, and then select Newsgroups from the pop-up menu. The Newsgroups window offers useful information about how newsgroups work in general, plus some specifics about using them through America Online. Take a few minutes to read through the documents there.

See also Part I for more information on using Parental Controls.

Posting messages to a newsgroup

A newsgroup audience is just waiting to hear what you have to say. Share your thoughts by posting a message. Before posting to a newsgroup, take time to read several days' worth of postings. Listen to what the members discuss and see how they do it. When you do speak up, make your posting appropriate for the newsgroup, both in topic and in tone. To post your message, just follow these steps:

1. In the Newsgroups window, click the Read My Newsgroups button. (If you're doing this offline, open the Filing Cabinet instead and go directly to Step 3.)

2. In the Read My Newsgroups window that opens, double-click the name of the newsgroup where you want to post a message.

3. Double-click any message inside the newsgroup destined for your message, and then click the New Message button. The Post New Message window appears.

4. Type your message into the Message text box, give it a Subject in the Subject text box; and then click the Send button.

If you're offline, click the Send Later button. After you finish writing messages, use Automatic AOL to post them.

See also Part V for more information about Automatic AOL.

Reading newsgroups online

After subscribing to a newsgroup, take time to read the messages. Here's how:

1. Use keyword **Newsgroups** to get into the Newsgroups window.

2. Click the Read My Newsgroups button. A window listing your newsgroups appears.

3. Double-click the newsgroup that you want to read. A list of unread newsgroup messages opens on-screen.

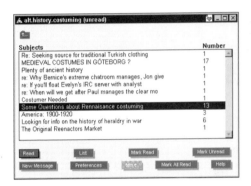

4. Scroll through the list until you find a message that looks interesting. Double-click to read it. The message appears.

5. When you finish with the message, close its window. Do likewise when you finish with the newsgroup.

See also "Reading newsgroups offline," "Remembering a newsgroup with Favorite Places," and "Replying to a newsgroup posting" later in this part.

Reading newsgroups offline

Newsgroups are fun and interesting, but they're also time consuming. Keep your phone line free by reading the newsgroups offline.

Reading the newsgroups offline is a two-step process. First, you configure the America Online software to read the newsgroups you want. Then you actually download the newsgroup messages and read and reply to them.

Setting up the software to read newsgroups offline takes only a few steps:

1. Subscribe to the newsgroups that you want to read offline.

If the newsgroup is extremely active, you may want to clear the posts by clicking the Read My Newsgroups button, highlighting the newsgroup in question, and clicking the Mark Read button. Then, when you download the newsgroup postings to your hard drive, you don't need to wade through 3,000 unread postings.

2. In the Newsgroups window, click the Read Offline button. The Choose Newsgroups window pops onto the screen.

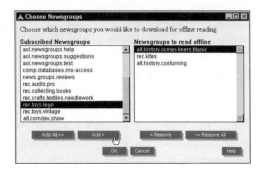

3. To read a newsgroup offline, double-click its entry in the Subscribed Newsgroups list. After a moment, the newsgroup hops to the Newsgroups to Read Offline list. Do this for all the newsgroups that you want to read offline.

If you double-click the wrong newsgroup or want to stop reading a newsgroup offline, double-click its entry in the Newsgroups to Read Offline list. The newsgroup returns to the regular Subscribed Newsgroups list.

4. When you finish, click OK. America Online returns you to the Newsgroups window.

5. To finish configuring America Online to retrieve your news-group messages for offline reading and replying, choose Mail⇨Automatic AOL. Select the check boxes beside these folders:

> Get unread postings and put in Incoming Postings
>
> Send postings from the Postings Waiting to Be Sent

6. Close the window when you finish.

Reading the newsgroups offline is a quick and easy process. Here's what you do:

1. Download newsgroup messages into your computer. Choose Mail⇨Automatic AOL to start an Automatic AOL session, just as you do to download your mail.

A small Automatic AOL Status dialog box appears and gives you play-by-play commentary as the Newsgroup messages come down the phone line into the Personal Filing Cabinet.

TIP

Stop by now and then to check the Automatic AOL process. If America Online decides that your newsgroups contain too many postings, it shuts down your Automatic AOL session with the terse message `Too many articles — download remaining articles in another Auto AOL (FlashSession)`. If that happens, begin another Automatic AOL session right away; the system happily downloads more postings into your computer.

2. To read and reply to the messages, choose File⇨Filing Cabinet.

3. Click the Newsgroups tab in the Filing Cabinet window that opens.

New messages are in the Incoming/Saved Postings folder. New messages are organized by subject line. Replies and new messages you write offline live in the Postings Waiting to Be Sent folder.

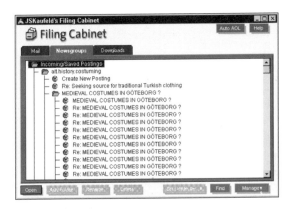

4. Double-click a message to read it.

See also "Replying to a newsgroup posting" later in this part.

Remembering a newsgroup with Favorite Places

If a particular newsgroup tweaks your fancy, store it in the Favorite Places list so that you can leap into it quickly. Here's how:

1. With a newsgroup window opens, click the heart-on-a-page icon in the window's upper right-hand corner.

2. Click the Add to Favorites button to add the newsgroup to your Favorite Places.

To access the newsgroup through Favorite Places, click the My Favorites button on the toolbar; then double-click the newsgroup's entry in the Favorite Places window. The newsgroup's window appears.

See also Part III for more information about Favorite Places.

Replying to a newsgroup posting

Newsgroups live for discussion. When something in a newsgroup piques your interest (or ire), add your opinion by posting a reply. Just follow these steps:

1. View the message to which you're replying.

2. Decide what kind of reply you want to send; then click the Reply button at the bottom of the window. The Post Responses window opens, showing the message in the Original Message text box.

3. Check the Post to Newsgroup option if everyone out there would find your words interesting. Do this only if your reply is part of an ongoing discussion. Check Send Via E-Mail if you have a specific question or if most of the newsgroup would yawn at the topic.

4. Write your reply into the Reply Window; then click the Send button.

The same steps work when reading your newsgroups offline — but remember to run Automatic AOL to send the reply when you finish reading.

See also "Reading newsgroups offline" elsewhere in this part.

Subscribing to a newsgroup

When a friend tells you about the cool pattern she found in `rec.crafts.textiles.needlework,` subscribe to the newsgroup with Expert Add — then check out the place for yourself.

You need to know the exact Internet name of any group you want to subscribe to. If you aren't sure of the name, use the newsgroup search feature I describe in the next section. To subscribe to any newsgroup, just follow these steps:

1. In the Newsgroups window, click the Expert Add button. The Expert Add dialog box appears.

2. In the Internet Name text box, type the name of the newsgroup that you want to join and then press Enter or click the Subscribe button.

3. After a moment, America Online either confirms your subscription or asks you to double-check the newsgroup name and try again. Either way, click OK to make the dialog box disappear.

See also "Reading newsgroups online" and "Reading newsgroups offline" elsewhere this part.

Searching for a particular topic

The America Online newsgroup search system covers most of the newsgroup hierarchies. It searches on the newsgroup name or parts of the name. To use the newsgroup search system, just follow these steps:

1. In the Newsgroups window, click the Search All Newsgroups button. The Search All Newsgroups dialog box appears.

2. Type a word or two describing your interest; then press Enter. After a moment, the search system proudly displays its results.

   If the system reports that it can't find anything, click OK and search for a different word.

To get the best results, search for one word or part of a word (*compu** instead of *computer,* for example). Remember, you're searching newsgroup titles, which are sometimes a little arcane. (An * after part of a word includes the letters typed plus anything else that the computer finds to insert in place of the asterisk. Thus, searching for `car*` could return car, cars, caroling, and carrot.)

3. Browse through the list and look for a newsgroup that interests you. Double-click a newsgroup's name to open the Add or Read Newsgroup window. This window lets you view a description of the newsgroup and read the newsgroup's postings or subscribe to the newsgroup.

   • **To subscribe to a newsgroup:** Click the Subscribe to Newsgroup link. A window opens with a list of unread postings. Double-click any posting title to open it.

   • **To read a newsgroup's postings without subscribing:** Click the List Articles in Newsgroup link. A list of the newsgroup's active articles appears in the same window that you see if you click the Subscribe to Newsgroup link. However, this time America Online shows the postings without actually subscribing you to the newsgroup.

4. Close any open newsgroup windows and the Add or Read Newsgroup window when you finish.

Browsing through the lists

Sometimes you're curious about what's out there. When those moments hit, browse through the newsgroup lists. With more than 13,000 newsgroups on the Net, you'd better bring your patience along for the trip. Here's how to browse through the newsgroup lists:

1. In the Newsgroups window, click the Add Newsgroups button. A list of newsgroup hierarchies appears. (See the hierarchy table at the beginning of the "Newsgroups" section for more information.)

2. Double-click a hierarchy that looks interesting. A list of newsgroups pops into view.

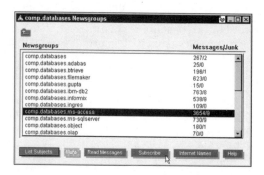

3. Scroll through the list and look for something that interests you.

   • **To see a listing of the newsgroup's articles:** Double-click the newsgroup's name; its window appears, listing active postings.

   • **To subscribe to a newsgroup:** Click the newsgroup name and then click the Subscribe button. If all goes well, America Online announces that you're subscribed. Click OK to make the dialog box go away.

4. Close the various windows when you finish.

Unsubscribing from a newsgroup

When it's time to say good-bye to a newsgroup, don't make it a long, drawn-out farewell. Just follow these steps:

1. Use keyword **Newsgroups** to open the Newsgroups window.

2. Click the Read My Newsgroups button. The Read My Newsgroups window appears.

3. Click the newsgroup that you want to remove from the list.

4. Click the Remove button. A dialog box confirms that you no longer subscribe to that newsgroup. Click OK to make the dialog box go away; then close the other newsgroup windows.

See also "Subscribing to a newsgroup" elsewhere in this part.

Search Systems on the Net

The Internet is a big place. The key to finding what you want is knowing where to look. These search systems make great starting points. Feel free to pencil in the addresses of other search systems as you find them. (After all, this is your book.)

Search System	Address
AltaVista	www.altavista.com
AOL Search	keyword **Search**
Excite	www.excite.com
Google	www.google.com
Go Network	www.go.com
Webcrawler	www.webcrawler.com
Yahoo!	www.yahoo.com

See also "Going to a specific Web site" later in this part.

Winsock Applications and AOL

In the world of Internet software, Winsock is a piece of programming that helps Windows applications interact with the Internet. Thanks to the America Online built-in Winsock support, you can use almost any standard Internet program through AOL, including Telnet, Internet Relay Chat (IRC), Gopher, and World Wide Web client applications.

AOL for Windows 95/98 (AOL 4.0 through AOL 7.0) supports a full 32-bit Winsock. This means that AOL for Windows 95/98 works with just about any Winsock-compatible program out there. For more details about using Winsock programs with AOL, plus a library of downloadable Winsock software, use keyword **AdvComp**. To find software, browse through the Advanced Computing Downloads section under the Features tab in the Advanced Computing Community window that opens. You're looking for the PC Internet Tools Libraries.

World Wide Web Adventures

Of all the information systems on the Internet, only one truly captured the public's imagination: the World Wide Web. With their flashy graphics, point-and-click interface, and limitless interlinks, Web sites are easily the Net's most popular destinations.

The America Online access software contains a powerful built-in Web browser. To hop on to the Web through America Online, simply type the Web address into the browser bar at the top of your AOL screen and click the Go button. The Web browser appears, displaying the AOL Web page. From there, you can browse the world's Web pages with ease.

Navigating the Web by clicking *links* in each Web page is easy. Links usually appear as colored, <u>underlined</u> text or as a graphic image on a Web page. When you move the mouse pointer over a link, the arrow changes into a pointing hand, indicating that you can click that link to view that Web page or document.

Your other navigational tools are the following buttons across the top of the browser bar:

✔ **Back:** Takes you to the last window you saw, not the last Web page you viewed.

✔ **Forward:** Takes you back where you were before you clicked Back.

✔ **Stop:** Cancels loading a Web page. Helpful when a Web page takes too long to load.

✔ **Reload:** Tells your browser to request a new copy of the Web page. Useful if something goes wrong while loading a page.

See also "Going to a specific Web site" later in this part.

Building a home page

In Internet lingo, a *home page* is your personal spot on the Web. A home page is a place to showcase your interests, promote your business, or expound the virtues of your particular viewpoint. What sets the Web apart is its worldwide reach — your words are available to anyone with a Web browser and Internet access.

For all the Web's power and reach, building a home page doesn't take a great deal of complex programming. In fact, putting your best foot forward on the Web doesn't take much programming at all. The key to this simplicity is the America Online 1-2-3 Publish (keyword **123 Publish**), an interactive tool that handles the technical stuff for you.

Making your own Web page

To create your own Web page using the America Online 1-2-3 Publish, follow these steps:

1. Use keyword **123 Publish** to open 1-2-3 Publish in the browser window. The screen fills with a list of template suggestions.

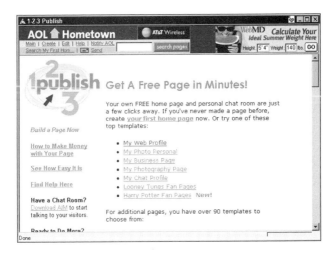

Decide what kind of Web page you have in mind. Do you want a page that showcases your baby's photos? Is this Web site's purpose to advertise your business? Would you like to post favorite recipes or share your delight over a television show? If ideas like these interest you, look for them (and more) in the item list.

2. Click a page template's link to select it. Then progress through the next screen's sections one at a time, entering a title for your Web page, selecting background colors, and including text.

   If you want to include a photo in your page design, you can do that, too. Click the Browse button to locate the picture or graphic. AOL uploads it automatically.

3. To see how the page will look after you enter all the information, click the Preview My Page button. If you want to change anything in your new page, click Modify while previewing it. To upload your page to AOL Hometown, the Web storage space that comes with your screen name, click Save.

For more advanced information on Web page construction, use keyword **Easy Designer**.

See also "Visiting friends at AOL Hometown" later in this part.

Get more in-depth information about America Online Web page design from *America Online For Dummies,* 8th Edition, by John Kaufeld (Hungry Minds, Inc.).

Going to a specific Web site

Use the browser bar's text box or the Keyword dialog box to quickly access any Web site on the Internet. Here's how:

1. Click the text box of the browser bar to highlight the text or choose Favorites⇨Go to Keyword to open the Keyword dialog box.

2. Type the address of the Web site into the text field; then press Enter or click Go (see in the Great Tapes figure where I enter **www.greattapes.com**). The built-in Web browser comes to life and begins loading the requested page.

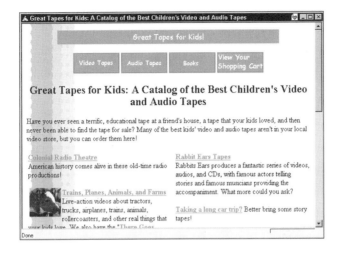

Using Microsoft Internet Explorer with AOL

The Netscape Navigator program's biggest challenger is from a small country — er, company — called Microsoft. Microsoft Internet Explorer (IE) software is duking it out with Netscape Navigator for dominance in the Internet marketplace. AOL adopted IE as its Web browsing software for the AOL programs for Windows 95/98. Whenever you see a Web browser appear inside this version of AOL, you're *actually* looking at Internet Explorer, even though the window looks just as it always did.

If you're really into surfing the Web, you can get faster Web response by running Internet Explorer *outside* of AOL. Just follow these steps:

1. Sign on to AOL.

2. Minimize the AOL window.

3. Find the Internet Explorer icon on your system (wherever it is) and double-click it. After a moment, Internet Explorer starts up.

4. Type the Web address you want to use into the browser's address box and enjoy!

Using Netscape Navigator with AOL

Netscape Navigator is one of the most popular Web browsers on the market. Luckily, Netscape Navigator is also a Winsock program. Because AOL supports Winsock programs, using Navigator with AOL is easy.

Netscape Navigator now comes packaged with an MP3 player, Netscape Radio, a Netscape version of AIM (AOL Instant Messenger), an e-mail program — plus a whole lot more. Look for this collection under the name Netscape 6. If you only want to download Netscape Navigator Stand-alone, which is the browser without all the extras, you can do that separately.

For all the details plus handy download libraries, use keyword **Netscape**.

Remembering a site through Favorite Places

With millions of sites available, you're bound to find a few best-loved locales on the Web. Use the Favorite Places system to keep them organized and easy to find. Just follow these steps:

1. Go to the Web site that you want to mark.

2. Click the Favorite Places icon (the heart on a sheet of paper in the upper right-hand corner of the window).

3. When America Online shows you its questioning dialog box, click Add to Favorites.

To go back to the page, click the Favorites toolbar button and then click the item's entry in the list.

Visiting friends at AOL Hometown

AOL Hometown is what America Online calls its members' Web page area. Completely free to America Online members, you can upload your Web page to AOL Hometown for other members to see — or spend an evening reading through other members' Web pages.

Divided into categories, AOL Hometown features member pages that discuss culture, entertainment, education, health, hobbies, and sports. AOL Hometown even contains a Business Park category for members who want to promote their businesses through a Web page.

Keyword **AOL Hometown** opens the AOL Hometown Welcome screen. Click the 123 Publish button to find out how to add your own Web page to the collection. To browse by general topic and subtopic, click the Site Map link. If you want to locate a specific topic or Web page, type this in the Search Pages text box.

Other Internet denizens who want to visit AOL Hometown (and who don't know your exact screen name) can see your page by using hometown.aol.com.

See also "Building a home page" earlier in this part.

Taking AOL on the Road

Thanks to more powerful and lighter laptops, computers are easy to take everywhere you go. As long as you're taking the computer with you, why not take America Online along as well? This part offers tips and techniques for making your online road trip as easy and painless as possible.

In this part . . .

Accessing Your Mail by Phone 154

Changing a Location 154

Connecting from a Hotel 155

Creating a Location 155

Creating a Location with Expert Add 158

Deleting a Location. 160

Finding a New Local Access Number 160

Making Location Entries 162

Signing On through the Internet 162

Signing On through Someone Else's Computer . . 163

Accessing Your Mail by Phone

You don't actually need access to a computer to find out what lies in your AOL online mailbox. If you subscribe to the optional AOLbyPhone service, you can check your mail, hear the latest news headlines, and see which movies might be playing in your area. Also hear weather reports for your immediate locale or your next destination.

Although AOLbyPhone is free to try, the service charges you $4.95 monthly after the first 30 days. AOL adds the fee to your credit card; if you try AOLbyPhone and then decide that you don't want to continue, you need to give the friendly AOLbyPhone people a call to cancel the service. Keyword **AOLbyPhone** gives you all the details.

Changing a Location

Making changes to a location is quick and easy. You may need to make a change like this to update your access numbers or reset your dialing options.

You might need to alter a location entry if:

- ✔ You move to a new location and want to change your home access number.

- ✔ The access number for your area changes.

- ✔ You upgrade your modem.

To change a location, follow these steps:

1. Start the America Online software but don't sign on to the system. In the Sign On window, click Setup. The America Online Setup window hops to attention.

2. Click the Expert Setup button. The Connection Setup dialog box appears on the screen. You should see a list of locations. If you see modem information instead, click the Locations tab.

3. Scroll through the location list until you find the location that needs an update. Click one of the Connection Profiles beneath it; then click the Edit button. The Edit Number (Connection) window for that profile rushes to the screen.

4. Make whatever changes are necessary.

5. Click OK to close the window and store the changes.

6. Click Close to close the Connection Setup window.

See also "Creating a Location," "Deleting a Location," and "Making Location Entries" later in this part.

Connecting from a Hotel

Success as a road warrior (today's equivalent of a samurai, a businessperson, and a nerd, all rolled into one) relies on good preparation. Before leaving on your trip, take a few moments to get everything ready. Here are a few guidelines:

- ✔ Find local access numbers for your destination and create locality entries for them (*see* "Creating a Location" elsewhere in this part). Because most hotels charge for each local phone call, this step alone may save you a few dollars.

- ✔ Create an entry for the America Online 800 number as a separate location. Although a small hourly fee is charged for using the number, it's far cheaper than dialing long distance or trying to explain your phone credit card number to the America Online software. The toll-free number for AOLNet is 1-800-716-0023. That connection is at 28.8 Kbps (kilobits per second) by the way. (Although the number itself is toll-free, AOL charges your credit card 10 cents a minute, or $6 an hour, to use the number.)

- ✔ Pack a connection tool kit. Don't worry — this isn't a particularly nerdy step. If you plan to sign on from many hotel rooms, though, you need the tools to do it. I wholeheartedly recommend purchasing a multipurpose Leatherman tool, available at sporting goods stores everywhere. *Note:* Check with any airline that you'll be traveling on before you try to board a plane or check luggage with any type of utility tool. I also recommend traveling with a couple of six-foot phone cords, a *splitter* (turns one jack into two), and a *mating plug* (connects your two short phone cords together to make a single long cord).

- ✔ Connecting around the world can be more art than science; be ready for some challenges. If your destination is outside the United States and Canada, you may need a phone jack converter and a voltage transformer. For online assistance, look to the International Access area (keyword **International Access**).

See also "Making Location Entries" later in this part.

Creating a Location

When you travel, the America Online access numbers change. Adding a new or additional dial-up location takes only a couple of moments, but it nullifies the frustration of landing in a new town and being unable to connect to AOL without a few costly hotel phone calls. Use these steps if you know that you want to create a new location, such as an entry for a travel destination. If you simply want to change the phone numbers that you use from your home computer, follow the steps in "Finding a New Local Access Number" later in this part.

Follow these steps to create a new location:

1. In the Sign On window, click Setup. The AOL Setup window pops onto the screen.

2. Click the Add Location button. The Add Location dialog box appears.

3. Type the location name in the aptly named Name box at the top of the dialog box. The AOL software helpfully suggests names such as Location 4; feel free to change it to something you'll remember — such as New York City or Cincinnati. Make sure that the radio button is selected next to *Select access numbers to add to my new location (recommended)*. Click the Next arrow.

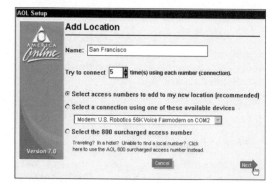

4. Enter the location's area code into the Search for AOL Access Numbers dialog box that appears. If you're creating a location for somewhere outside the United States, click the down-arrow next to Country and select the country's name from the pull-down menu that appears. For countries outside the United States, you don't need to worry about the area code. When you're ready, click the Next button to continue.

5. The friendly Select AOL Access Phone Numbers window appears with a list of access numbers matching the area code you enter (or the country you select). The new location you create in Step 3 appears in the Add Numbers to This Location list. In the AOL Access Phone Numbers list, check the phone

number(s) that appear(s) next to your destination city. Click the Next arrow to continue.

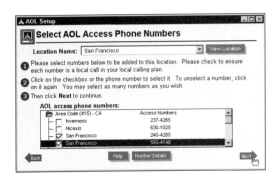

Selecting more than one access number gives the software a choice if one of the numbers returns a busy signal or is unavailable when you attempt to connect.

6. The Confirm Your Selections dialog box appears, warning you that your modem dials the new numbers without the area code. If that's all right with you, click the Next arrow.

If, for some reason, your modem needs to dial the area code before the local access number for your new location, click the Edit button and check the *Dial area code* option.

Select the items at the bottom of the Confirm Your Selections dialog box to put in any special dialing instructions (such as reaching an outside line or disabling call waiting). If your phone system uses numerals other than 9 for an outside line and *70 to disable call waiting, select the appropriate option and then change the command in the numeral's text box.

If you create the location for travel purposes, be sure to ask at the front desk about any unusual phone codes that patrons might need to access an outside line. It saves possible frustration later.

7. Click the Next arrow in the Confirm Your Selections dialog box when you finish. The system then asks you to Confirm Current Location numbers. If all looks right to you, click the Finish button. The window disappears, and the Sign On window reappears. Your new location is ready to use. To sign on to America Online immediately by using the new access numbers, click the Sign On button instead of closing the window.

If you're creating entries today with a future trip in mind, make sure to select your home location from the Select Location list before you try to sign on to the service again. Otherwise, AOL helpfully attempts to sign on with the location you just created and its not-so-local phone numbers.

See also "Finding a New Local Access Number" later in this part.

Creating a Location with Expert Add

The Expert Add setup option bypasses the step-by-step help and enters your information directly into one window. To use Expert Add, you need to know the access numbers that you plan to use. One way to find them is to use keyword **Access** to search for access numbers in the United States or keyword **International Access** to search for a number worldwide. With list in hand, you're ready to use Expert Add. Just follow these steps:

1. Make sure you're offline to add a location. Click the Setup button on the Sign On window, and the America Online Setup window appears.

2. Click the Expert Setup button. The Connection Setup window appears, displaying an active Locations tab.

3. Click the Expert Add button. The Add Number (Connection) dialog box appears.

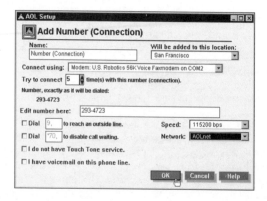

4. If you want to replace the default Number (Connection) with a city name or more useful term, type the name of your new profile into the Name box at the top of the window. Then press Tab.

5. Choose the new entry's location from the *Will be added to this location* box. If you're creating a new location with this entry, choose *Add to new location*. Then press Tab.

6. If the software correctly identifies your modem, press Tab. If not, correct the entry in the *Connect using* box and then press Tab.

7. Click the up-arrow next to *Try to connect X time(s) with this number (connection)*. Setting the number to 5 or above makes the software retry several times when it reaches a busy signal before it moves to the next access number.

8. Select the *Edit number here* box and carefully type the first local access number. If you have to dial 1 and the area code, put those in as well.

9. Click the down-arrow next to Speed and then pick the appropriate modem speed from the list. Most AOLNet access numbers use 28.8 or 33.6 Kbps; some SprintNet numbers still use 14.4 Kbps.

10. Unless you know that the number that you have uses SprintNet or some other access network, leave the Network box set to AOLNet.

11. By default, dialing is set to touch-tone. If you're using a pulse phone, select *I do not have touch tone service*.

12. To include any special dialing instructions (to dial a number to reach an outside line or to disable call waiting), select the appropriate check boxes at the bottom left of the window.

If your phone system uses something other than 9 for an outside line or *70 to disable call waiting, just select that setting and change the command.

13. Take a last look to make sure that everything you've entered is correct and then click OK. You return to the Connection Setup window.

14. Click Close to shut the window. To create another access number profile for your location, repeat Steps 2 through 13.

When you opt to add the access number to a new location, the Connection Setup window automatically names your entry Location and tacks a number onto the end of it. If you desire a less computerese title for your new location, highlight the Location under the Locations tab in the Connection Setup window, and click Edit. In the Edit window, erase Location, replace it with the name you've chosen, and then click OK. Your location's name proudly takes its place in the Connection Setup window.

Deleting a Location

Saddled with too many locations? No problem — just delete the ones you don't need. Here's how:

1. In the Sign On window, click Setup. The America Online Setup window hops onto the screen.

2. Click Expert Setup. The Connection Setup window appears. You should be looking at the Locations tab contents. If not, click the Locations tab to make it active.

3. Scroll through the location list until you find a location that you don't need anymore. Click once to highlight that entry.

4. Click Delete.

Finding a New Local Access Number

America Online makes finding new local access numbers very easy — far simpler than any other online service I've ever used (and that's saying something).

Access numbers are built right into the software. Instead of signing on, finding access numbers, and writing them down, you can do the whole access number thing offline. (Of course, if you *like* to do it the hard way, you can find access numbers online at keyword **Access**.)

To find a new access number, follow these steps:

1. Start the America Online software but don't sign on to the system.

2. Click Setup at the bottom of the Sign On window. The AOL Setup dialog box appears.

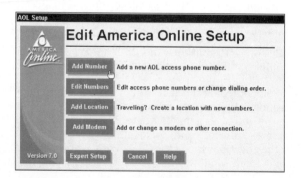

3. Click the Add Number button. A Search for AOL Access Numbers dialog box hops to attention.

4. To search for an access number in the United States, enter the location's area code. To find a number for another country, click the arrow in the Country text box and choose from the nations listed. Click the Next arrow. The Select AOL Access Phone Numbers window appears.

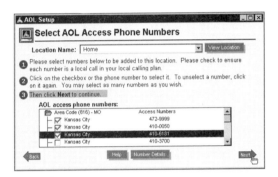

5. Check the phone number(s) you want to use in the AOL Access Phone Numbers list. Then click the Next arrow.

If you want the numbers to go into a unique location for travel, you want to create a new location. *See* "Making Location Entries," later in this part, for the lowdown.

6. After you click the Next arrow to place the access number in your home location, the Confirm Your Selections dialog box pops up to remind you that your modem will dial the number without the area code. If that's okay with you, click the Next arrow. On the other hand, if you want your modem to use the area code for some reason, click an Edit button and make your changes. Then click the Next arrow.

If you're calling through a phone system that requires you to dial 9 for an outside line, select the check box beside *Dial 9 to reach an outside line*. Likewise, to disable call waiting, select the check box beside *Dial *70 to turn off call waiting*. If the numbers 9 and 70 don't match the system you use, replace them with your code numbers — but leave the commas after the numbers. The comma tells the phone system to pause between the first set of numbers and the phone number.

Confirm Your Selections

Your modem will dial these access phone numbers **exactly** as shown.
If necessary, click on the **Edit** button to modify how the number will be dialed.
If you need to add or remove a number click on the **Back** button.

Access Numbers You've Selected

1)	Edit	472-9999	Kansas City, MO, Area Code 816.
2)	Edit	410-0050	Kansas City, MO, Area Code 816.
3)	Edit	410-6181	Kansas City, MO, Area Code 816.

☐ Dial 9. to reach an outside line.

☐ Dial *70, to turn off call waiting.

Back   Help   Next

7. If you want to get access numbers for another part of the country or the world, click the Back arrow in the lower left-hand corner of the Select AOL Access Phone Numbers window and repeat the selection process.

8. When you finish choosing your new numbers, click the Finish button. You find yourself back at the America Online Sign On dialog box. To use your new numbers right away, click the Sign On button at the bottom of the Select AOL Access Phone Numbers dialog box. AOL uses your new numbers to sign you on to the system.

That's it — your new access entry is ready to go.

Making Location Entries

America Online provides local phone numbers all over the United States, Canada, and the rest of the world. The AOL software organizes these access numbers with location entries. Each location stores two access phone numbers, plus dialing instructions, such as pressing 9 for an outside line and *70 to disable call waiting. Because the America Online software remembers multiple locations, the more you take America Online with you on the road, the easier connecting becomes.

You need to sign off from America Online before working with the location entries in your software because you can only access the dialog boxes from the Sign On window.

Signing On through the Internet

Any time that you're close to a computer connected to the Internet, you have access to your America Online account. This feature is called AOL Anywhere, and it makes connecting to your account easy and painless, no matter where you happen to be.

Here's how it works: You find yourself at a conference, visiting at a business office, or in the university computing lab. (Or sitting in an Internet Café in Ghana, for that matter — this little trick works there, too.)

To use AOL Anywhere:

1. Sidle up to an Internet-accessible computer and visit www. aol.com. On the main AOL page, you see an AOL Members Sign On section.

2. Type your screen name and password into the Screen Name and Enter password textboxes, and then click the Sign On button. America Online welcomes you.

3. Select any of the AOL Anywhere features by clicking its button. You can read your e-mail, check your online portfolio, read news and more with My AOL, or consult the AOL Calendar.

When you finish, be sure to click the Screen Name sign-out button — especially if you're on a public computer. America Online then signs you off the private part of its system and tells you that you've been successfully signed out of AOL Anywhere.

Signing On through Someone Else's Computer

Although this technique *sounds* slightly illegal, it's actually a very easy and valuable option that's built right into the America Online software.

Here's the scenario: You're on the road visiting some friends (possibly people you met through America Online). During the visit, you get a sudden urge to check your electronic mail. Their software, of course, contains only *their* screen names, not yours. That's where the Guest option comes in.

By signing on as a guest, you use your chum's software with *your* screen name and password. Any online charges for the session go to your account, as always. Some limitations exist, though: You can't use Auto AOL, create Favorite Place entries, switch screen names, or access the Download Manager. Other than those limitations, the world (or at least America Online) is your oyster.

To sign on as a guest, follow these steps:

1. In the Sign On screen, click the down-arrow next to Select Screen Name. Click the Guest screen name. The Password box disappears but that's normal behavior for a Password box (seems they're never around when you need them).

2. **Click the Sign On button to connect with America Online.**
   The process moves along smoothly until the Checking Your
   Password stage. At that point, the Guest Sign-On box appears.

3. **Type your screen name and password into the appropriate
   boxes and press Enter or click OK.** If you spelled everything
   correctly, America Online welcomes you with open arms.

Solving Problems and Finding Help

Although the online world is a great deal of fun, it also provides more than a few confusing moments. That's why America Online offers many places to turn for help and consolation in your time of trouble. This part is your road map to help. Use the information here when you know that something's wrong but you aren't sure where to turn. Best of all, most of the options in here are free of connect charges if you subscribe to an hourly usage plan.

In this part . . .

Adding Your Own Two Cents Worth 166

AOL Help 166

AOL Tray Icon 167

Billing Problems 168

Calling America Online for Help 169

Finding a Lost Window 169

Free Help from Other Members 169

Freeing Up Some Virtual Space 170

Get Help Now 172

Host Not Responding 172

Lost Carrier 173

World Wide Web Page Won't Load 174

Adding Your Own Two Cents Worth

If you like something, don't like something, or just want America Online to change something about its services, take a minute to make your voice heard! To send comments and suggestions to various America Online content areas, use keyword **Suggestions**. (It's even free!)

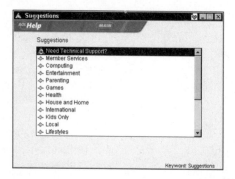

1. Double-click the channel name or content area.

2. Enter your comment into the text field.

3. Click Send.

AOL Help

America Online provides free help to members in the AOL Help area (keyword **Help**). Questions about America Online itself, online accounts, and billing find answers in AOL Help. Plus, you find information on everything from downloads to chat areas and from online safety to the Internet. Free of connect-time charges, this area is designed to offer members information about AOL. You can also press F1 for AOL Help.

✔ Click any of the subject links to begin drilling down to helpful information. Each subject link that you click hones the topic a little more; look in the item list for the articles that correspond to a particular topic.

✔ Enter a search topic into the text box at the top of the AOL Help window and click the Search button to bring up a list of possible topics. Double-click an entry to read the article.

✔ Use the AOL System Status window to learn about any system-wide information you should know, such as scheduled maintenance downtimes, a list of cities receiving additional capacity or access numbers, and any new phone numbers that you might need (such as the additional toll-free access number). Use keyword **AOL Update** to open this window.

AOL Tray Icon

If you call America Online technical support for help, you may be asked to do something with the AOL tray icon. This icon, which rests in the lower right-hand corner of your screen on the Windows taskbar (in what computer geeks call the *system tray*), provides loads of technical information about your computer — what type of processor your machine has, how much memory it contains, and other helpful tidbits. A supremely helpful feature, the AOL tray icon reveals exactly the kind of system information that AOL technical support might need if you ever call with problems.

To view the system information, you don't even have to be signed on to AOL. Here's how to use the tray icon:

1. Right-click the AOL icon in the System Tray. A small menu appears.

2. Choose System Information. The AOL System Information dialog box appears, listing the version of AOL loaded on your system, your available memory, browser information, and much more.

If you don't see the AOL icon in your System Tray, you can still get to the information. Here's how:

1. Click the Start button in the Windows taskbar.

2. Choose Programs from the menu that appears.

3. Choose America Online from the Programs menu.

4. Select AOL System Information.

Billing Problems

If you need to check your current bill and find the answers to billing questions, keyword **Billing** takes you there. Time spent in this area is free of online charges.

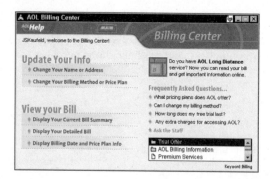

Use this area to

✔ Check your current bill summary

✔ Change your name or address with America Online

✔ Change your billing method and information

✔ Read the answers to questions most often asked about America Online billing

To request credit for a download that went awry or an evening when the America Online computers didn't feel like talking to you, use keyword **Credit**. Only members who use America Online's measured service would ever need to use the Credit window.

Calling America Online for Help

Most of the time, you can find help about America Online while connected to the service. Sometimes, though, connecting to AOL *is* the problem. In that case, you need some human help. Talk to a live technical support staff member at 1-800-827-3338. If possible, be near the computer when you call (the technician may need to know some specific info about your computer).

Here are the toll-free numbers you need to contact America Online:

✔ For general technical help, call 1-800-346-3704.

✔ To talk to the sales staff, use 1-800-827-6364.

✔ TTY users call 1-800-759-3323.

See also "AOL Tray Icon" in this part.

Finding a Lost Window

The windows that contain AOL's various online areas often get buried in the flurry of online activity. And, of course, the window hiding on the very bottom of the pile is the one you need to see. Fear not — that's why those clever America Online programmers created the Window menu:

1. To quickly find the lost window, click the Window item in the menu bar. A menu drops down, just as you expect it to. The bottom of the menu lists the first nine open windows, and the item marked with a check is the active (or top) window on your screen.

2. If the window that you want is on the list, click its entry. Immediately, that window pops to the top of the pile.

If the window you want *isn't* on the list, choose Window⇨More Windows to see a complete window list. Scroll through the list and double-click the window that you need.

For a quick look at where you've been, even if you closed the window, click the down-arrow on the browser bar. A list drops down from the bar, listing the last 20 or more windows you opened while online. Click one of them, and that window opens on-screen.

Free Help from Other Members

Who knows America Online better than your fellow members? Nobody! Some of the best help on the whole system is available from other people, like yourself, in the AOL Help Community area.

This area is only a keyword away — and it won't cost you a penny to access it. Browse the AOL Help Community message board for answers to questions on billing, e-mail, uploading files, and more:

1. Use keyword **Help Community** to open the AOL Help Community window.

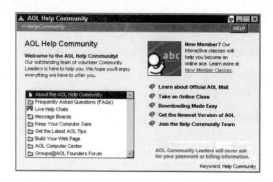

2. Double-click the Live Help Chats or Message Boards entries to open windows that lead to boards and chats.

3. Click the <u>AOL for Windows</u> or <u>AOL for Mac</u> link, depending on the type of computer you have.

See also Part VI for more on discussion boards.

Freeing Up Some Virtual Space

If you download files with abandon, use your Filing Cabinet to its fullest potential, and visit Web sites by the hour, sooner or later you might receive a dialog box declaring that your resources are dangerously low, or that your Personal Filing Cabinet is so full that it's slowing down your AOL experience. Taking action before you see these dismal dialog boxes keeps your America Online software running smoothly and your computer happy.

Reducing the Personal Filing Cabinet

Delete unnecessary e-mail messages that you've downloaded using Automatic AOL. Get rid of the newsgroup postings that you've read or the postings contained in message threads that don't interest you. The software will run better when you reduce the amount of stuff that AOL needs to load each time you open it.

Here's how to clean out your filing cabinet:

1. Choose Mail➪Filing Cabinet from the toolbar. Your Filing Cabinet window opens.

2. To delete a particular message or posting, highlight it and click the Delete button. To get rid of an entire folder's contents, highlight the folder and click the Delete button.

3. America Online throws a dialog box to the screen that asks whether you really want to do this. Click the Yes button to delete the item or folder and close the dialog box, all in one smooth motion.

 If you *don't* see a dialog box that asks whether you want to delete the items, use keyword **Preferences** to set your Filing Cabinet preferences to *Confirm before deleting single items* and *Confirm before deleting multiple items*. On the other hand, if you're trying to delete several items at once and you get tired of clicking Yes, use the Filing Cabinet preferences to turn *off* the confirmation messages.

If you delete many files from the Filing Cabinet, a dialog box appears that asks whether you want to compact your Filing Cabinet and reclaim the space for your hard drive. Compacting your Filing Cabinet is an America Online term for compressing the files on your hard drive. Click the Compact Now button to provide more free space for your computer.

Purge cache: AOL Tray icon

The Web browser keeps track of where you've been online. Many online denizens visit the same Web sites over and over again. Keeping the sites that you visit loaded into your browser cache significantly reduces the amount of time needed to load the page a second time.

If you visit a *lot* of Web sites, however, an overstuffed browser cache can bog down response time during your online sessions. Here's how to delete those files and gain the virtual space again:

 1. Right-click the AOL tray icon. Look for it in the Windows taskbar system tray — next to the clock in the lower-right corner of your screen.

2. Select System Information from the menu that appears. An AOL System Information dialog box opens on screen.

3. Click the Utilities tab.

4. Click the Clear Browser Cache button.

5. Click the Close button.

Get Help Now

Get help with your computer and America Online through the Computer Center's Get Help Now window. Here you can link to nightly Help Desk chats, where live volunteers answer your computer questions. Open any folder or document you find here to learn about everything from creating a new folder in Windows to Online Safety & Security. Use keyword **Get Help Now** to open the window.

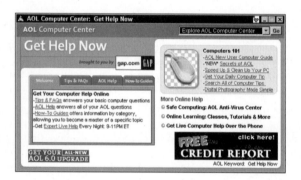

Host Not Responding

Sometimes, the America Online computers get snippy and ignore you for no apparent reason. The hourglass appears and you wait . . . and wait . . . until a dialog box tersely informs you that the *host* (a fancy term for the big America Online computers) is not responding.

Most often, this happens when the online system (AOL's system or the Internet) is extremely busy, but sometimes a more insidious problem may exist. If you get such a message often, the culprit may be line noise from the modem line or a bad modem setting. Consider:

✔ **Before working yourself into a lather over the problem, try your request again.** Most of the time, the computers didn't get around to your request yet. Giving them another opportunity solves the problem.

✔ **Modems, like all the other technologically sophisticated widgets in your life, get confused sometimes.** Resetting the little gadgets is the only way to bring them back to their senses. If you use an external modem (a small box that sits outside the computer), find the modem's power switch and turn it off for about 15 seconds; then flip the modem on and try again. If you have an internal modem (one lurking inside your computer), shut down your computer for about 20 seconds, and then restart it. Such a shutdown not only gives the computer a fresh outlook on life, but it also completely resets the modem.

✔ **If resetting the modem doesn't fix the problem, then you may have a noisy phone line.** Phone line noise frequently comes and goes, but if the problem persists, call your local phone company and ask someone to check your line for interference.

Lost Carrier

One moment the connection to America Online is fine and the next moment you're no longer connected. This abrupt loss of service is called *lost carrier* (or being "punted," in AOL members' lingo, as in, "What happened to you?" "Oh, I got punted."). Members may also refer to it as "being dropped."

Usually, random line noise causes the lost connection. Unfortunately, you can't do anything about that — random line noise is just part of online life. Simply sign on to the service again and continue with your regularly scheduled online life.

If the problem happens often, though, check your modem settings to make sure that they're correct. To check the modem's settings:

1. Before signing on to America Online, click the Setup button at the bottom of the Sign On window. The America Online Setup window appears.

2. Click the Expert Setup button. The Connection Setup window jumps to the screen, awaiting your bidding.

3. Click the Devices tab.

4. Highlight your modem and then click the Edit button. A somewhat imposing list of modems pops up.

5. Scroll through the list until you find your modem; click that entry once. If you aren't sure what kind of modem you have, choose Hayes compatible (error-correcting); it works with most modems.

6. Click OK to close the Modem Selection list. Then click Close to close the Connection Setup window.

Sometimes you can get dropped even if you don't use a dial-up modem. If you connect to AOL via an Internet connection of some kind (see the Bring Your Own Access area, keyword **BYOA**, for more information), you might occasionally lose your connection and see a message box that states that the TCP/IP has lost the connection because the network subsystem has failed. When you see this, try waiting a moment or two and then sign on again. That usually fixes the problem.

If your connection still doesn't work the way you think it should, try contacting America Online technical support for more help.

See also "Calling America Online for Help" earlier in this part.

World Wide Web Page Won't Load

Cruise the Web, find Internet treasures yet unexplored, and join the cyber-travelers of the new millennium. All this sounds terrific, right up to the point when the Web page refuses to load. Often, a line of text appears reading `Error 404` is to blame. This error, to strip away the mystique of large numbers, simply means that the Web page won't load.

A Web page that refuses to load is a very common problem that you may encounter when surfing the Web. Try the address later and see whether the Web page appears then. Frequently, the Web page loads after a wait and a second try.

Places of Our Hearts

America Online has so many wonderful areas that I simply had to share some with you. This part contains some favorites — a complete listing would take many more pages (yes, I probably do need to get out more). Each of the favorites in this section includes the area's keyword so you can find it and take a firsthand look.

If some of these become "Places of Your Heart," store them in your Favorite Places list. When you find an online area that's too good to lose, click the heart icon in the upper right-hand corner of the forum's screen. When AOL asks whether you want to add the location to your Favorites, click Yes. Then you've got it — your new Favorite Place is saved.

(**See also** Part II for more about adding Favorite Places.)

Ages & Stages

Want to connect with other adults your age? Whether you call yourself collegiate, a 20-something, a senior citizen, or something in between, you'll find message boards, chats, and features devoted to your stage of life in the Ages & Stages area. Links in this area lead to travel options, Web page communities, some history resources, and a couple download libraries.

Keyword: **Ages & Stages**

AOL Hometown

AOL Hometown organizes members' Web pages by category. Use this area to visit AOL member Web sites or upload your Web page for others to enjoy. If you run a business and want to advertise your wares or services, upload your page to AOL Hometown's Business Park category. Or wander through the Business Park to see what other AOL members offer in products and services.

Keyword: **Hometown**

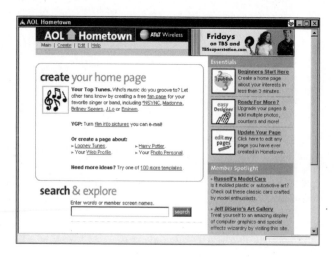

Billing Center

Beginning in December 1996, America Online offered a new unlimited-usage plan that currently costs $23.90 per month. (The world rejoiced except for the credit card companies that lost revenue.) Although keeping track of your bill isn't quite as important as it used to be under the hour-by-hour plan, it's still wise to check your charges every now and then — especially if you play America Online's Premium Games. Visit the Billing area for all this info and more.

Keyword: **Billing**

Build Your Web Page

Build Your Web Page helps you design your own killer Web page — with information about the personal Web storage space that comes with every AOL account, 1-2-3 Publish and Easy Designer (programs that help you make the easiest use of your personal Web space), and live classes nearly every weekday evening. Think of Build Your Web Page as your personal path to an Internet image.

Keyword: **Web Page**

Celebrities

Find out who's doing what in the Entertainment channel Celebrities window. Check out celebrity transcripts from online chats, read celeb interviews, or jump to Entertainment Weekly, People.com, or E! Online. Wherever you like to get your news of the rich, famous, and stellar, you'll probably find a link to it from the Celebrities window.

Keyword: **Celebrities**

Conspiracies and UFOs

If you're one of the people who think that a CIA-backed extraterrestrial shot John F. Kennedy, then you may enjoy a trip through ParaScope. This area specializes in conspiracy theories, the paranormal, and the unusual. ParaScope contains an interesting library of downloadable documents. Check it out. It's out there.

Keyword: **ParaScope**

Daily Byte

Fill your hard drive one file at a time or wax poetic over your new computer tip in the Daily Byte area. One quick stop gives you a daily file for your hard drive, creation for the printer, and technology article. Stop by and see what the technoweenies planned just for you.

Keyword: **Daily Byte**

Dilbert Zone

Turn to the Dilbert Zone for a daily chuckle. Catch up on office humor, submit your suggestions for the List of the Day, and begin the day with a giggle. If you ever want to know what computer nerds are really like on a day-by-day basis, Dilbert comes pretty close.

Keyword: **Dilbert.com**

Evening Essentials

The next time that you want to wind down with AOL — before you wander home from work or maybe after dinner — try the Evening Essentials window. Here you find the evening's sports listing, end of the day market news, commuting information, and the television listings. Check out recent news photos or read a movie review. By the time you decide what to do with the rest of the evening, you'll be prepared.

Keyword: **Evening Essentials**

Explore

This feature appeals to the little kid in all of us who loves surprises. Enter keyword **Explore** and the Explore window opens, sitting quietly in the lower right-hand corner of the screen and displays a roulette wheel. Click the wheel, watch the wheel spin, and poof! An America Online screen opens before your eyes. Browse the area or close the new screen and click the wheel again. Explore never tires of sending you to new areas for your exploration.

Keyword: **Explore**

Food & Recipes

Who doesn't like a good meal every now and then? In the AOL Food & Recipes area, you can unearth enough new ideas to serve an innovative meal every night. Look here for gourmet recipes, worldwide cuisine, healthful treats, veggie specialties, and more. Locate and then save your favorite recipes online, print coupons to take to the grocery, or browse through dinner suggestions.

Keyword: **Food**

Learning Network

Whether you follow your son's kindergarten studies, your daughter's college courses, or the many stages in-between, you'll enjoy the Learning Network. This site discusses hot topics and current parenting issues. The focus is family education and teaching resources; you can also find family activities, trends in education, and specialized options (such as gifted-and-talented programs and homeschooling tips) here.

Keyword: **Learning Network**

Games

Game shows, trivia, role play, classic strategy . . . AOL Games plays it all and provides forums to discuss most of it. Use the item list to browse available areas. The EA Lounge takes you to trivia and puzzles, in addition to game shows.

Keyword: **Games**

History

Discover the past in the American History or World History sections, reading the biographies of famous individuals, or looking into the history of war and espionage around the world. Each section offers articles, message boards, and chats.

Keyword: **History**

Homeschooling

Interested in taking a look what's new in the homeschooling movement? Then drop by the Homeschooling section of the Parenting Community. With active message boards and regularly scheduled chats, the forum keeps America Online homeschoolers informed.

Keyword: **Homeschooling**

Homework Help

Need an answer to a classroom assignment? America Online's Homework Help area may have the solution. In this area, students ask questions of volunteer tutors in a live chat room. Or you can post your question on the subject message boards. If you're in the mood to browse, use the Look Up Answers link to find Web sites and text documents that match your homework question.

Keyword: **Homework Help**

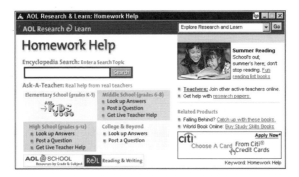

International

Fix yourself a cup of tea or coffee and settle back for a worldwide experience. The World of AOL now includes Argentina, Australia, Austria, Canada, France, Germany, Japan, Latin America, Mexico, Sweden, Switzerland, and the United Kingdom, and are they neat! Browse to your heart's content, but don't be surprised if you stumble upon a forum or two written in the native language. Click the continent that interests you; as the mouse hovers over any portion of the map, a list appears to show you that continent's active America Online versions.

Keyword: **International**

My News

Set up a news profile to capture the news that really interests you and save time browsing the front page. The My News profile grabs the topics you want to read about and delivers them to you. And you don't have to worry about missing the front porch — the stories land squarely in your e-mail box, every time.

Keyword: **My News**

The New York Times on AOL

Missing out on grabbing *The New York Times* from your mailbox each morning? Although it won't fill your lap, you can get the day's news from America Online. Read daily news as well as stories about technology, religion, current local events, and health. The Times site also provides a look at the past for students in the

Learning Network section. The Times offers a crosswords subscription service; for a small fee you can enjoy the celebrated Times puzzle on your computer (or off) each day.

Keyword: **Times**

Notify AOL

Sometimes, sad to say, obnoxiously behaving people gain access to the America Online chat rooms. If you find yourself plagued with one of these folks and this person has gone over the edge of obnoxiousness into a blatant Terms of Service (TOS) violation, use Notify AOL to file a report with the AOL cyberpolice. Use the Chat button in the Notify AOL window to report chat room problems. Notify AOL also provides a place to report violations in Instant Messages, Web sites, message boards, or screen names.

Keyword: **Notify AOL**

O2 Simplify

For those times when you feel you need to cut back, O2 Simplify (part of the AOL Women's Channel) offers helpful articles on home care and organization, the kids, travel, work, and more. While you're here, you also might want to check out the related articles on the Ka-Ching site, which talks about women and money (keyword **Ka Ching**), or Moms Online (keyword **MomsOnline**).

Keyword: **O2 Simplify**

Radio@AOL

Listen to your favorite music style while you browse the Internet or hang out in the AOL chat rooms. With this new feature from America Online, you choose from over 100 programmed stations. Select Just 4 Kids to amuse the little ones at your house or explore the latest sounds in Latin Jazz. Whether your heart quickens at the sound of classical, country, or chart toppers, you'll find a station just for you. If you hear a song that sparks memories and you want a copy for yourself, the Radio@AOL window conveniently provides a CDNow button so that you can purchase the album online. The easiest way to open the Radio@AOL window is to click the Radio button on the AOL toolbar.

Keyword: **Radio**

Science

Use the Science area as a springboard to some wonderful forums that focus on science. Planet Earth, Space, Nature & Wildlife, Archaeology, and 21st Century Science resources, including several science Web sites and current science news, are only a click away.

Keyword: **Science**

What's New

Save time by going directly to a listing of the newest, coolest, or hottest areas of America Online. Some of the forums listed are new, some are really neat, and others qualify for the "you really need to know this exists" category. They change often, so check back once in a while to see the latest and greatest online destinations.

Keyword: **New**

Where Were You When . . .

Where were you when . . . JFK died? Nixon resigned from office? Elvis died? Check into the Where Were You When area every now and then and relive your past. This forum highlights the news stories that touched our hearts and our lives — the ones that people are still talking about 10, 20, even 30 years or more later. Read the histories, browse the memories — even post your own remembrances.

Keyword: **Where Were You When**

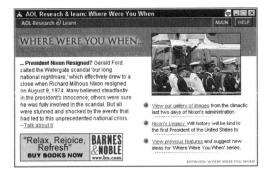

Who Am I?

How's your sense of history and your knowledge of the people who played a part in it? Each week, Who Am I? profiles a famous person. Read the description, see whether you know who it is, and then use the online encyclopedia link to learn more about that person.

Keyword: **Who Am I**

Your Favorite Team

No matter who plays on your best team — or what they play, for that matter — you can use the team's name or nickname to go directly to the group's window on AOL. Here you'll find a roster, schedules, stats, attendance comparisons, and more. To visit the New York Knicks area, for instance, use keyword **Knicks**. After you get the hang of it, you might find that it's easier to use the team name as a keyword than it is to track that window through your Favorite Places list.

Keyword: **your favorite team's name or nickname**

Clicking through the Channels

If any one place is truly the crossroads of America Online, it's the Channels list. This window is your ticket to the system's 21 main content channels. When you're looking for something new to do or someplace cool to go, the Channels list is *definitely* the place to begin. From this one screen, you can journey to the farthest reaches of AOL, exploring all kinds of new and exotic areas as you go.

To help you along the way, this appendix offers a quick overview of the various channels. Here, you find some basic information about each channel, including tips about content and specific things that you don't want to miss. Each channel has departments that are easy to locate, whether by clicking a button, using the Search & Explore feature, or by typing a keyword that's similar to the department's name (look for examples in the Channel sections). Jot down notes about your favorites!

Welcome

When you want to know what's happening online today, drop by the Welcome window and see. Welcome highlights the most current information from News, Health, Entertainment, Personal Finance, and many of the other channels. The window's contents change every day or so. As your first stop each time that you sign on to AOL, the Welcome window provides links to your city's weather and late-breaking news — not to mention your e-mail, You've Got Pictures, and the AOL Calendar.

Autos

If you're looking for a new car or want some tips on fixing up your current vehicle, Autos is the place for you. Here you can work through a car buyer's decision guide to narrow your choices for those new (or slightly well-loved) wheels, find out about insurance, and complete an online finance calculator to see how much you can afford for car payments.

Nestled under the Talk About Cars link in the main Autos window, you'll find buttons that lead to Car & Driver Online (keyword **Car and Driver**), Road and Track (keyword **Roadandtrack**), and Driving Today (keyword **Driving Today**).

Click the Maintain Your Car link in the main Autos window to navigate through car basics such as changing a tire and jump-starting a car. While you're here, take an under-the-hood tour, dip into the illustrated repair guide, or take a peek at the Vehicle checklist. It leads to a Preventative Maintenance Check List that helps you keep on top of repairs before they become emergencies.

Like all the other channels, Autos also offers a thriving set of discussion boards and a 24-hour chat room. You can share your love of cars and cycles — or your questions — with other members any time (keyword **Autos Community**).

Careers & Work

If you work for a living (and I don't know anybody who doesn't), you'll find lots of good information in Careers & Work. Whether you want to begin a career, start a home business, or you're happy right where you are, this channel provides resources, tips, and a great place to hang out after five (and it's a lot cheaper than a night in the bars).

Eight departments (plus the channel's Explore Your Profession option) help you find the information you need. Salary and Benefits (keyword **Salary and Benefits**) helps you figure out where you fit into the sliding scale. Take the Career Finder quiz (keyword **Career Finder**) to see which potential jobs match your interests the best. Improve Yourself (keyword **Improve Yourself**) offers tips for presenting yourself — and your ideas. To find out about other companies, have a look at Research a Company. Start-Up Businesses (keyword **StartUp**) provides resources for business owners. If you want to discuss work and work environments matter-of-factly, try Career Talk (keyword **Career Talk**); for the heads-up on available career training and online education, click the Professional Training button (keyword **Online Campus**. Research a Company (keyword **Research a Company**) gives you opinions from inside the corporations you might be considering. The last department, Find a Job, leads you to online employment listings and resume generators.

Even with all these departments, locating business areas online is not easy. My best picks include Business Week Online (keyword **BW**), Business Tools & Reference (keyword **Tools & Reference**), and Start-Up Businesses (keyword **StartUp**). For overall business, technology, and financial-market updates, you can browse Business News (keyword **Business News**).

Computer Center

Whether you use a Macintosh or Windows computer, you can find a home in the computing channel. The area features information on all aspects of computing, including work, play, art, and music. The channel's main buttons lead you into the various focus areas, including Print Central, the Internet, Hardware and Software, and a *humongous* downloadable file library.

The channel's support area, Get Help Now, is your direct link to friendly people and message boards — live support chats, informative documents, and a dictionary of computer terms.

Finally, be sure to take a peek into Fun Stuff. Here's where you find computer game helps and news, the Daily Download, and a link to the Computer Community (keyword **Computing Communities**).

Favorites here include the PDA area (keyword **PDA**) where you can get all kinds of tips, downloads, and conversation pertaining to your favorite personal digital assistant; Print Central (keyword **Print Central**), which links you to printable projects for holidays, home, school, and office; and Get Help Now (keyword **Get Help Now**), an area full of computing secrets and how-to information.

Entertainment

Hooray for Hollywood — and also for AOL's version of the fantasy and tinsel factory, the Entertainment channel. If you want movie scuttlebutt, TV trivia, music news, or just Dave Letterman's latest Top 10 list, begin your search here. The channel's main window links you to entertainment-oriented areas, both within AOL and out on the World Wide Web.

The channel offers eight main areas: Movies, Music, Television, Celebrities, Community (message boards and chat rooms), Books & Arts, Going Out, and Fun & Games. The Search section helps you locate areas within Entertainment if you can't find them under the department buttons.

Games

Fun knows no bounds, particularly in this most fun of all online places: the Games channel. Gamers of all ages find things to do, people to meet, and conversations to join here in the Grand Central Station of good times.

Of course, the Games channel covers lots and lots of computer games — but don't assume that the fun stops there. Board games, fantasy role-playing games, sports games, and strategy games all take their rightful place in this channel as well. You can even choose from several online games that let you play head-to-head against other AOL members.

The Games window leads to five focus areas organized by game type. The Word & Puzzle button leads to crosswords, word searches, and more. Free Casino & Lottery takes you to gambling-style games, and Card & Board sends you into the classic online games such as checkers and Hearts. Arcade, Trivia, & More acts as a catch-all compartment for those games that don't fit anywhere else. EA Games sends you to games that run the gamut from Bunny Luv to Silent Death Online. EA Sports, on the other hand, specializes in soccer, baseball, and other sports games.

To locate your favorite game genres online, use the See All Games button and browse the alphabetical list of links that appears. Most of the online games cost nothing to play. A few of them fall under the Electronic Arts Platinum Service, which you can sign up for an online subscription for $9.99 per month and then you play as many of the Platinum Service games as you want each month with no additional hourly surcharge.

Health

Healthy living is a hot topic for almost everyone these days. When your mind fills with questions about eating right, finding a support group, or living an active lifestyle, the Health channel is ready with information, discussion, shopping, and more.

The Health channel has these categories: Diseases & Conditions; Dieting & Nutrition; Fitness & Exercise; Alternative Medicine; an Online Pharmacy; Doctors & Health Plans; Health & Beauty; and Health News; and four categories for the health concerns of special groups: Women, Men, Children, and Seniors.

Each category spotlights an aspect of health, and each contains specialized forums, articles, and links to Web sites. Select a topic and wander through the folders until you find something you like.

House & Home

Click the House & Home channel button when you're looking for information on decorating, home life, or leisure activities. This channel's thirteen departments are divided into two separate categories: Living and Housing.

Living includes, Decorating, Food & Recipes, Gardening, Home Improvement, and Pets. Housing includes the Real Estate Center, Mortgages, Moving, Neighborhoods, and Renting.

If you enjoy a particular home-related interest, such as sewing, try using it as a keyword. The area that you're looking for might open immediately, saving you a browse through the various House & Home windows.

International

If you long to travel the world but your budget suggests a quick trip around the block, then try the International channel. It's the next best thing to grabbing your passport — plus you don't have to wait in any lines at the airport.

The International channel's main feature is the country-specific areas — you have hundreds to choose from! Each area includes both AOL-based information and World Wide Web links. Many countries have discussion boards as well. Whether you're planning a vacation or simply interested in a particular far-off (or not-so-far-off) land, these areas are information-packed places to start. Just click the appropriate continent on the International channel map and then double-click the country you want to investigate.

For a more interactive experience, check out AOL's international versions. As of this writing, you can take a look at what AOL members see in Argentina, Austria, Canada, France, Germany, Japan, Latin America, Mexico, Sweden, Switzerland, and the United Kingdom. Just hover the mouse over the world map; a pull-down menu appears listing any active AOL versions in the various continents. Click on the foreign AOL version's continent; then click whichever international AOL area you want to see on the individual continent's map that appears. This feature is particularly valuable for foreign language students because the content in the foreign areas appears in the country's native language.

Kids Only

Sometimes, AOL seems to be just for grown-ups. Kids need a place to call their own, too! And that's exactly why AOL created the Kids Only channel. This channel is devoted exclusively to activities, information, and all-around fun for kids. Grown-ups need not apply!

The goal of the Kids Only channel is to create a safe haven for kids to explore and interact. The channel offers educational areas, online games, clubs, sports talk, weather, and places to take youthful creativity for a spin. Because the Internet contains so much valuable information, Kids Only also includes a bunch of kid-safe Web links.

As a parent, you can feel pretty comfortable about letting your online kids play here. The Kids Only staffers take their jobs very seriously. Their priority is providing kids with a safe and valuable online experience — which they do quite well.

Remember that you can limit your child's screen name to only allow access to Kids Only if you want. To find out the details, check out the Parental Controls at keyword **Parental Controls**.

See also Part I for more information on Parental Controls.

Local Guide

What channel is a cross between an atlas, a travelogue, and a do-it-yourself guidebook? You guessed it — Local Guide! If you're looking for information about a particular city in these United States, this is definitely a great place to start.

The Local Guide channel features all kinds of details about cities all over the United States. In addition to the standard travel-oriented fare, you can find discussion boards and chat rooms for debating topics of local interest — whether you're a visitor or a full-time resident.

To find out what's available online for various cities in the United States, click the Visit Another City link. From the AOL Local Guide: Main — Make It Your Town window that opens, enter a new city and state name or a new five-digit zip code, and then click the Go button.

Another way to browse the Local Guide is to select a topic of interest from the main window, such as Arts & Culture, Dining, Health,

Kids & Family, Movies, News & Sports, or Visitor's Guide. Then
select your preferred city from the list that appears.

If you really enjoy this channel, take a look at both the International
and Travel channels as well.

Music

Whether you sway to Big Band, move to Hip-Hop, or line dance to
Country, you'll find your favorite genre in the Music channel. Use
the Find Music Styles department name to reveal your favorite type
of music in a pull-down menu, and you can listen to samples of several recent releases, buy featured CDs online, or catch up with
genre scuttlebutt.

Also use the Music channel when you want to follow music news,
chat or trade messages about your favorite artists, or explore
Internet Radio. Internet Radio brings music through your computer
via your online connection. With an Internet Radio player like
Spinner, you can select from over a hundred different music channels and listen while you work (or play.) Keyword **Internet Radio**
takes you directly to the Internet Radio window.

News

Of all the AOL channel windows, News probably gets the most traffic. In addition to its spot on the Channels menu, News is where you
land when you click the Top News Story button on the Welcome
window.

Eleven sections make up the News window. They are Nation,
Business News, World, Health News, Entertainment News, Family
News, Life: The Lighter Side, Weather, Sports, Photos, and Local.
For a general trip through the channel, click any of the top story
headlines or click on a headline in the quick news summary ticker.

To make finding specific stories even easier, AOL created the My
News profile system (keyword **My News**). After you try out My
News profiles, you won't ever want to do news the old-fashioned
way again.

Parenting

AOL has long maintained its dedication to computing families, and
now they have a channel of their own. In the Parenting channel, you
find parenting helps, parental controls, and a host of other resources
designed to make your life a little easier. Use the departments to
delve into information for all phases of family life: Pregnancy, Family

Issues, Genealogy, Family Entertainment, Mom-to-Mom, and Dads. Babies, Preschoolers (ages 3 to 5), Grade Schoolers, and Teens complete the Parenting by Age lineup at the top of the screen.

In addition, use the Search text box at the top of the window to help you find specific information inside the Families channel. Some of the best family areas online include Parent Soup (keyword **Parent Soup**), Parenting.com (keyword **Parent Time**), and the Learning Network (keyword **Learning Network**).

Personal Finance

For tips and conversation about investing, stocks, and other greenback-related topics, drop by the Personal Finance channel. As the name implies, this is where all the monetary details hang out between economic shifts (and even during them).

The Personal Finance channel is organized into departments and financial centers. Departments include My Portfolios, Market News Center, Business News, Banking & Loans, Stocks, Real Estate, Mutual Funds, My Account Manager, and Planning. The channel's top picks include The Motley Fool (keyword **Motley Fool**) and the Investment Research area (keyword **Company Research**).

Beware as you tread through the channel, though. Many of the investment areas are sponsored by companies who want to do business with you. Although these companies probably won't lie to you outright, they'll certainly try to put the best possible spin on the truth. You'll do just fine in the channel if you write down the old adage "Don't believe everything you read" in big letters and keep it near your monitor every time you visit this channel. (Don't say I didn't warn you.)

Research & Learn

The Research & Learn channel brings you the best in online education and reference information. This channel is a smorgasbord of cool places, stemming from three broad categories:

Research: Resources covering nearly any topic you can imagine

Learn: Covers things such as homework help, subject areas, and neat stuff for parents and teachers

The Research & Learn window organizes all this information under three headings: Reference, Subjects, and Education. Reference leads you to online dictionaries, encyclopedias, and the like, and Subjects takes you to forums and reference material for topics such as history, science, business, education, and geography. Education provides information on professional training, college, and financial aid.

A top pick here is the White and Yellow Pages (click the White and Yellow Pages button under Reference). These searchable national directories are a gold mine of information. Best of all, there's no extra charge to use them. (Life just doesn't get much better than this.)

Shopping

Thanks to AOL's lush shopping channel, now you don't even have to go to the mall to indulge in America's favorite pastime. (Your credit card company thanks AOL profusely, no doubt.)

The Shopping channel is organized into 18 areas. The main areas lead you to Web pages, which offer choices in the various categories. If you want a specific store, try using that store's name as a keyword — or look for it in the A–Z Store Directory.

Sports

If following various balls, wheels, pucks, clubs, and flags stirs your soul, then the Sports channel is sure to be a favorite stop for you. It's chock-full of statistics, discussion, and conversation about sports from auto rallies to the ones at the other end of the alphabet (you know, zebra racing), plus lots of others in the middle.

The Sports window offers two different ways to dive into the details. To focus on a particular sport, click the appropriately named button in the middle of the window. If you're interested in scores, discussions, or fan-related gatherings, use the Scores or Team Pages buttons on the window's left-hand side. Keyword **Sports Community** takes you to the heart of the discussions, where you find message boards, sports-related chats, and more.

Teens

Where do you go to find the latest sound, homework help, and rockin' chat rooms all at the same time? The Teens channel, of course. No longer buried within another channel's territory, teens now have their own channel hangout, just like Kids Only.

You'll find the Teens channel divided into the major categories in a teenager's existence: Music, Movies & T.V., Celeb Fan Club, Games, Sports, Girls, Real Life, Chat & Boards, and Style. These sections practically explode with chat rooms, message boards, articles, and opinions. If you're looking for a place to meet other teens and share what's on your mind, you'll love the Teen channel.

Travel

See the world and swap stories with other travelers in the Travel channel, the online home of people who explore the world (and those that want to). From travel plans to travelogues, this channel has it all.

Three buttons vie for your attention at the left-hand side of the channel window. Destination Guides leads to a cool window that helps you develop travel ideas based on your interests and other members' stories. Interests & Activities collects travel information around topics such as adventure travel, theme parks, cruises, family travel, and more. Hot Deals helps you pick out specific destinations and activities based on available bargains and money-saving ideas.

On the other side of the screen, the Fares & Reservations list puts you in touch with online travel specialists who make your dream vacation a reality (just have your credit card number handy)!

Check out the other buttons in the window for general tips and discussion in the travel board. My personal pick is the Resources & Tips area (keyword **Resources & Tips**). Here you'll find everything from information on international phone calls to luggage guidelines, all in one place. Also check out the Weather area (keyword **Weather**) because it always pays to know what you're getting into before you go. (Memories of a very cold arrival in Calgary, Alberta keep this tip warm in my mind.)

Women

AOL's new Women channel explores women's interests, events, and lifestyles. Whether you (or the women in your life) are interested in Beauty & Fashion, Relationships, Wellness, Weddings, Living, Money & Work, or just hanging out in Women Talk, this is the place to be.

Especially useful are the large buttons at the bottom of the window. Clicking these takes you to Women.com, Oxygen, iVillage.com, and Oprah Online — four wonderful areas dedicated to women, their lives, and their needs.

If you're looking for something to do, try the AOL Women Activities area, at keyword **Women's Activities**. Use the Women's Features area to read up on important issues, such as depression, working at home, or surviving trauma. Keyword **Women's Features**.

Glossary: Tech Talk

AOL Globalnet Plus: If you live outside the United States, America Online created its international communications system, AOLGlobalnet Plus, just for you. Using AOL Globalnet incurs a surcharge of $6 to $24 per hour, depending on what country you live in. Keyword **International Access** tells more.

AOL Hometown: Look for America Online members' personal Web pages at AOL Hometown. This area stores and categorizes the Web pages that members create with the free Web space that comes with each America Online account. Keyword **Hometown** tells how you can become involved, too.

AOLnet: Similar to AOL Globalnet, AOLnet is America Online's North American communications system. America Online members pay nothing extra to use AOLnet, unless they use the AOL 1-800 access number. Use keyword **Access** to find out more about accessing America Online through AOLnet.

Automatic AOL: Why sit around waiting for America Online to download or upload messages for you? When you schedule an Automatic AOL Session, AOL automatically signs you on at a predetermined time, downloads or uploads the messages or files you specify, and then signs off.

Calendar: You can set your America Online Calendar to notify you of music releases, international holidays, daily weather, you own appointment schedule — practically whatever makes your world go 'round. After you take the time to set up the Calendar, you can even print monthly or daily pages to help you keep it all together. Keyword **Calendar** takes you there.

Channels: Channels organize America Online's content area into broad categories. Click a channel button alongside the left side of the screen to see what's under that channel's heading; use the Search feature to search for a particular topic within all the channels.

chat rooms: Chat rooms are interactive windows on America Online. Most chat rooms live under the People Connection channel, but you can also find them in content areas. When in a chat room, members type comments, press Enter, and watch the line of text appear in a large, scrolling window for everyone in the chat room to see.

content: Content refers to online information areas within AOL. Also known as content areas, online areas, or forums, you use keywords, the Channels buttons, or the Search feature to get to AOL content. Content areas are the heart and soul of America Online.

cookies: In the past, even on the Net, cookies referred to those wonderful baked treats with gooey chocolate chips and nuts. Now, in regard to the Net, cookies mean tiny files that Web pages sometimes deposit in your Web browser's "sites you've visited" collection. These files contain information — such as any passwords you use to access the site, your preferences while you were there, and maybe your order selections if you purchased anything from the site. This way, your likes and dislikes remain where they should — on your computer system — and not on some computer in cyberspace.

discussion board: Message boards within content areas on America Online are known as discussion boards. Members post messages in order to discuss topics, and other members reply or comment. Discussion boards exist under almost every content area.

download: Bringing a file from America Online or the Internet into your computer is called downloading. To mark files for downloading, tell AOL to download the files now or later; check the files marked for downloading under File⇨Download Manager.

e-mail: Electronic mail, or e-mail, enables people to communicate back and forth by sending messages to e-mail addresses either through America Online or out to the Internet. (Not to be confused with the term snail mail, which Internet denizens use to refer to regular postal service.)

emoticons: *See* smilies.

EXE files: A file with the extension .exe does something. Unlike text in document files, executable files run on the computer. EXE files usually contain a program of some kind. You need to be wary of downloading these files from e-mail if you don't know the sender.

Favorite Places: Mark a special spot on AOL with the Favorite Places feature. This feature gives you a white page icon featuring a red heart (in the corner of most America Online windows) that you can use to create a shortcut back to a special place. Eventually you create a Favorite Places list that you can view by choosing Favorites⇨Favorite Places.

free area: Any time you're in a part of America Online that accumulates no connect time charges, such as AOL Help, you're visiting a free area on the service. America Online kindly lets you know when you enter and exit a designated free area. This applies only if your price plan charges you by the hour of online use rather than the common $23.90 for unlimited connect time each month.

FTP (File Transfer Protocol): If you find a really great file on the Internet, you use FTP to download it. FTP is the Internet standard for uploading and downloading files and graphics. Use keyword **FTP** to give it a try.

Groups@AOL: Groups@AOL is what America Online calls the private discussion board areas that members create. Available to members age 18 and over, these online communities can be used to track an organization's events, coordinate family members, or explore (and share) a favorite topic among friends. Use keyword **Groups** to find out more.

HTML: HyperText Markup Language, or HTML, is the computer code you use to create Web pages. Web browsers turn a Web page's HTML code into the formatted text, color, and graphics you've come to know and love. `<B>Welcome!</B>` is an example of HTML code — in this case, an instruction to the browser to display **Welcome!** onscreen in bold text.

IM (Instant Message): Little windows pop up on-screen with messages from friends and strangers. These are known as IMs, or Instant Messages. You can send and receive Instant Messages when you are signed on to America Online. You can't send an IM from a free area, although Instant Messages are visible in free areas and you can read them there.

Instant Messenger: With Instant Messenger (also known as AIM), you can communicate with friends on the Internet via Instant Message windows. Your friend downloads the Instant Messenger software and creates a screen name that America Online understands. Place that screen name in your Buddy List and AOL lets you know when your friend is on the Net. Keyword **Instant Messenger** gives you the details.

Internet: The worldwide network of networks is called the Internet. Not specifically a place, the Internet allows computers to talk to each other without national barriers. FTP, the World Wide Web, e-mail, mailing lists, and Usenet newsgroups are all part of the Internet.

Internet Explorer: Internet Explorer is the built-in Web browser that America Online uses to link you to the Internet. Designed by Microsoft, Internet Explorer works seamlessly with Windows and is built into Windows 98 and above. You may also hear it called MSIE (short for Microsoft Internet Explorer).

Internet radio: Although you can listen to many local radio stations via the Web these days (an Internet search using the call letters of your favorite station will tell you if it's online), the term Internet radio actually refers to pre-selected "stations" that focus on rock, jazz, big band, alternative, world rock, and other specific music genres. You download the Internet player, select your favorites, and listen to music piped through your AOL connection. Although it works best with a fast connection such as a cable modem, you can still enjoy Internet radio with a 56 Kbps modem. Keyword **Internet Radio** tells you more.

Internet Service Provider: An Internet Service Provider, or ISP, is the company you use to access the Internet. When you use AOL, your ISP is America Online (although AOL provides a lot more that actually makes it an online service). Most ISPs provide e-mail, FTP, and a Web browser. You can't access America Online's content through an ISP unless you're an AOL member. Keyword **BYOA** explains Bring Your Own Access (connecting to America Online through an ISP).

keyword: Keywords are code names that offer shortcuts to most areas on America Online. To use a keyword, press Ctrl+K (or click the Keyword button), enter the keyword, and press Enter. Keywords in this book are printed in boldface type.

lurking: Hanging out in a chat room without responding to any of the scrolling conversation is known as lurking. This word has its origin on the Net, where people often join newsgroups or mailing lists and read for months at a time without introducing themselves. It's considered a little rude to lurk without at least saying hello, in both environments.

mailing list: Members who belong to a mailing list write electronic mail (about a specific topic) that goes to everyone else on the list. Conversations evolve as members send their comments to the mailing list's e-mail address. Many AOL channels offer their own mailing lists.

master screen name: Master screen names carry more power than ordinary screen names. The first screen name that you create on America Online is a master screen name, but you can also designate any other screen name that you create as a master screen name. Only master screen names can set Parental Controls and change billing options. The other screen names in an account are secondary screen names.

menu bar: The top of the screen sports a row of words: File, Edit, Print, Window, Sign Off, and Help. This bar full of words is called the menu bar. Click any of these words and a list of items (a menu) appears under the menu heading. Click one of the items to activate that command.

modem: The piece of equipment that allows your computer to talk over the phone line is called a modem. Modems may be internal, fitting into a slot inside the computer itself, or they may be external. External modems plug into the backs of computers (like printers do) and allow you to watch lights flash as they connect to America Online and send and receive information. (Although a cable connection is called a *cable modem*, it's actually a constant active connection with an Internet service provider rather than a modem per se.)

My News: You can set up My News profiles to drop news articles — about topics you're interested in — right into your e-mail box. Use keyword **My News** to set up a profile for your account.

newsgroups: Track an interest through an Internet Usenet newsgroup. These worldwide discussion boards each cover one small topic, and you can check them out through America Online. Keyword **Newsgroups**.

offline: Any time that your computer and America Online aren't actively connected, the computer is said to be offline.

online: After your modem calls America Online, you've entered your password, and the Welcome screen appears, you're online. Online is the term used when a computer talks to another computer via modems.

primary screen name: The first screen name that you create on your America Online account is considered the primary screen name. You cannot change or delete your primary screen name; if you decide you hate it three months into your account, your best bet is to create another screen name that you do like on the account and use it instead. Your primary screen name carries master screen name status. *See also* master screen name.

profile: Information about yourself that you provide for other America Online members to read is called a profile. Profiles give a snapshot view of who you are. The profile form offers space for your name, city, hobbies, favorite quote, and more; enter as much or as little information as you like. Some profiles list only first name and city; others offer tidbits about the person behind the screen name. See keyword **Profile** and then click the My Profile button.

scammer: People who send official-looking Instant Messages in an effort to fish for passwords are known as scammers. *Never provide personal information to anyone who sends an Instant Message asking for password or credit card numbers,* but do report them by using the Notify AOL button at the bottom of the Instant Message window. (No AOL staff person will ever ask for your password.)

screen name: Your screen name is your America Online member name as well as the name by which others know you on America Online. Add @aol.com and the screen name becomes an Internet e-mail address.

smilies: Those little keystroke faces — ;) :> 0:) — are known as smilies (or emoticons). Used to spice up e-mail, chat room chatter, and Instant Messages, these shorthand faces bring a smile (or a frown) to everyday conversation.

toolbar: Under the menu items at the top of the screen lurks a toolbar — a row of icons that stretches from one side of the screen to the other. Click one of the icons to go somewhere on America Online or to reveal a menu of choices. Move the mouse pointer over an icon to find out what the icon does.

Winsock: Winsock is the little piece of magic that makes Netscape Navigator and your other favorite Internet software work through America Online. The term itself is short for Windows sockets, which are behind-the-scenes software hooks for Windows-based Internet programs.

World Wide Web: Although it's only one part of the Internet, the World Wide Web receives the most attention and airplay. Also called the Web or WWW, this Internet area contains text and graphics that are combined to present information in files known as Web pages. To see a Web page, you have to enter the exact Internet address into the Web browser or use the address as a keyword. To get started, click the text field on the browser bar at the top of your screen, enter the Web address, and click Go to use America Online's built-in Web browser.

You've Got Pictures: You've Got Pictures is a collaboration effort between Kodak and America Online. When you have photos developed, you can elect to have your pictures placed online in your AOL You've Got Pictures area. Then, in addition to the prints and negatives, you have scanned photos that you can use for e-mail and purchased photo gifts. Use keyword **Pictures** to get started.

ZIP: The most common kind of compressed file on America Online ends with a .zip extension. These are (you guessed it) ZIP files, often created with programs such as PKZIP or WinZip. A single ZIP file may contain one program or several all smashed together. Compressing a bunch of stuff into a ZIP file makes uploading and downloading faster. To open (or unzip) a ZIP file, you need PKZIP, WinZip, or a compatible program. The America Online software itself understands ZIP files and attempts to unzip them automatically after downloading.

Index

Symbols and Numerics

:: (double colons), 48
! (exclamation point), 38
( ) (parentheses), 75
? (question mark), 38
//roll command, 49
{S command, 47
1-2-3 Publish, 149, 177
123 Publish keyword, 149
800 AOLNet phone number, 155

A

abbreviations. See shorthand
Access keyword, 158, 160, 195
access numbers. See also location, dial-up
    changing, 154
    international, 155, 158, 195
    local, finding, 160–162
    new, finding, 167
    for North America, 155, 195
    toll-free number, 155
    for travel destination, 155–158, 158–160
Activity Group, in Groups@AOL, 98
Add2Cal keyword, 17
Address Book
    adding Buddies to, 54, 60
    adding entries to, 68–69
    auto-suggesting e-mail addresses, 7, 94
    auto-suggesting screen names, 65–66
    changing or removing entries in, 70
    groups in, 68–69, 70
    sending e-mail messages from, 94
Address Book option, Mail menu, 68
AdvComp keyword, 147–148
advertising, restricting, 7–8
AG keyword, 88
age. See also children; Parental Controls
    online areas for specific age groups, 176, 183, 193
    setting for screen name, 11–12
Ages & Stages keyword, 176
albums. See also pictures
    adding pictures to, 110
    changing, 108–109
    creating, 109–111
    creating Buddy Albums, 115
    creating from Buddy Albums, 111–112
    deleting pictures from, 110
    layout for, 110
    receiving Buddy Albums, 113–114
    sharing Buddy Albums, 115–117

all caps, avoiding, 50, 80
AltaVista search system, 147
Alternative newsgroup topics, 139
America Online 7.0 For Dummies (Kaufeld), 4, 14, 27, 64, 124, 150
America Online icon, BP-7
American Greetings Web site, 87–88
Anonymous FTP. See FTP
Anti-Virus center, 134
AOL Anywhere, 162–163
AOL Community Action Team, 50, 63, 85
AOL Globalnet Plus, 195
AOL Help, BP-10, 166–167. See also help
AOL Help button, BP-7. See also help
AOL Help Community, 169–170. See also help
AOL Help window. See also help
AOL Hometown, 14, 152, 176, 195
AOL Hometown keyword, 152
AOL Live keyword, 42
AOL Media Player, 8
AOL Protocol, chat room guidelines, 38
AOL screen, BP-2–BP-3
AOL Search, BP-14, 30, 147
AOL tray icon, 167–168, 171
AOL Update keyword, 167
AOLNet, 155, 195
appointment planning. See My Calendar
arenas, 38–39
art, online. See graphics
Association preferences, 4
attachments
    downloading, 4, 72–73, 122
    receiving in an e-mail message, 85–86
    sending with e-mail message, 70–72
    viruses in, 123
Automatic AOL
    definition of, 195
    preferences for, 4, 72–73
    reading newsgroup messages, 142–143
    running immediately, 73, 91
    scheduling, 73–74
    storing passwords for, 74
Automatic AOL option, Mail menu, 91, 142–143
Autos channel, 186
Autos Community keyword, 186
auto-suggesting e-mail addresses, 7, 94
auto-suggesting screen names, 65–66
Away Message, 56–57

B

Back button, on browser bar, 148
background color, e-mail, 82–83, 85
background image, in e-mail, 82
BCC (blind carbon copies), 75–76
billing
    getting information about, 176–177
    problems with, 168
    screen names with permissions for, 10
Billing keyword, 168, 176–177
blind carbon copies, of e-mail, 75–76
blue border and envelope on e-mail, 85
bold text. *See* formatting
bookmarks. *See* Favorite Places
boxes. *See* check boxes; dialog boxes; text boxes
Bring Your Own Access (BYOA), 173–174, 198
browser bar, 36, 148–149
browser cache, purging, 171
browsers, 151–152
browsing the World Wide Web, 148–149, 151–152
Buddy Albums
    creating, 115
    creating albums from, 111–112
    receiving, 113–114
    sharing, 115–117
Buddy Chat room, 39, 57–59
Buddy keyword, 54, 56, 59, 65
Buddy List
    adding Buddies to Address Book, 54
    adding friends to, 54, 56
    on AOL screen, BP-3
    Away Message for, 56–57
    description of, 55
    getting information about Buddies, 60
    groups in, changing, 56
    groups in, creating, 59
    groups in, deleting, 59–60
    locating Buddies, 44–45, 60
    preferences for, 9, 65–66
    removing Buddies from, 56
    sending Instant Messages in, 65
    sounds for, 9, 65
Business News keyword, 187
Business Park in AOL Hometown, 152, 176
buttons, BP-4, BP-5. *See also specific buttons*; toolbar
BW keyword, 187
BYOA keyword, 173–174, 198

C

cache, browser, 171
Calendar. *See* My Calendar
Calendar button, BP-7
Calendar keyword, 15, 195
capital letters, avoiding, 50, 80
captions, displaying with multimedia, 8
Car and Driver keyword, 186
carbon copies, of e-mail, 75–76
Career Finder keyword, 187
Career Talk keyword, 187
Careers & Work channel, 186–187
carrier, lost, 173–174
cars, online areas about, 186
Case, Steve, e-mail messages from, 85
CBS News keyword, BP-12
CC (carbon copies), 75–76
CD player, setting default, 8
celebrities, online areas about, 177, 184, 187–188
Celebrities keyword, 177
centering text. *See* formatting
channels
    browsing, 26–27
    Communities based on, 43
    descriptions of, 185–194, 195
    entering disscussion boards through, 96
    for My Place destinations, BP-9, 35
Channels list, BP-2, 26–27, 185
Chat button, BP-6
Chat option, People menu, 46
chat room
    alphabetizing member list in, 5
    Buddy Chat room, 39, 57–59
    definition of, 195
    etiquette guidelines for, 50–51
    fonts and formatting in, 5, 38, 48
    ignoring someone in, 51
    locating, 42, 44–45
    logging for, BP-11, 126–128
    member chat room, 39–40, 42
    Parental Controls for, 22
    in People Connection, 38, 46
    People Here list in, 51
    preferences for, 5
    presentations in, 38
    private chat room, 40
    reading Member Profiles in, 49
    role-playing in, 48–49
    rolling dice in, 49
    safety issues in, 49–52
    sounds in, 5, 47
    types of, 38–39

Chat Schedule keyword, 42
check boxes, BP-4, BP-5
children. *See also* education
    Health channel, Children's area, 189
    Homeschooling keyword, 180
    Homework Help keyword, 180
    Kids Only channel, 190
    Learning Network keyword, 179
    Parental Controls for. *See* Parental Controls
    Parenting Channel, 191–192
    Radio keyword, Just 4 Kids option, 182
    screen names for, 10
    Teens channel, 193
    Trusted and Restricted Sites for, 6
Coliseum, 39
:: (colons, double), 48
colors. *See also* formatting
    background in e-mail messages, 82–83
    of links, 6
    of official AOL mail, 85
    of text in chat rooms, 38, 48
    of text in e-mail messages, 82–83
comments, making to AOL, 166
communications system
    international (AOL Globalnet Plus), 155, 158,
        195
    for North America (AOLnet), 155, 195
Communities keyword, 43, 129
Company Research keyword, 192. *See also*
    Research a Company keyword
Computer Center channel, 187
Computer Center Get Help Now, BP-10, 172,
    187
computers, newsgroups about, 139
computers, online area about, 178, 187
Computing Communities keyword, 187
connection tool kit, 155
conspiracies, online area about, 177–178
content, definition of, 195
content areas. *See* online areas
cookies, defintion of, 196
Copyright keyword, 136
corporate e-mail messages, 85
credit card requests, 62–63
Credit keyword, 168
credit refunds, 168
customer support phone number, BP-8, 169

D

Daily Byte keyword, 178
developing pictures, 112–113
dialog boxes, BP-4–BP-5
dial-up location
    changing, 154
    creating, 155–158, 158–160

deleting, 160
description of, 162
dice, rolling, 49
dictionary for spell-checking, 9
digital photos, 117–119
Dilbert.com keyword, 178
Direct Marketing Association Mail
    Preference Service, 8
directory. *See also* folders
    for downloaded files, 5, 73, 122
    for sound files, 47
discussion areas. *See* Groups@AOL
discussion boards
    accessing, 101, 104
    description of, 100–101, 196
    finding new messages in, 96
    preferences for, 103–104
    private and public discussion areas. *See*
        Groups@AOL
    reading messages in, 104
    replying to messages in, 102–103, 105
discussion groups. *See* Groups@AOL
disk icon, 85
disk space, for online art, 6
:: (double colons), 48
Download Center keyword, 126
Download Manager
    confirming before adding files to, 5
    destination directory, setting, 122
    downloading files from, 122, 125
    downloading FTP files with, 136
    file descriptions in, 122
    putting e-mail attachments in, 122
    putting files from file libraries in, 125
    removing files from, 123
    viewing downloaded files in, 129
    viewing files in, 123
Download Manager keyword, 122
Download Manager option, File menu, 122,
    123, 196
downloading attachments, 4, 72–73, 122
downloading e-mail, 4, 72
downloading files
    with Automatic AOL, 73
    decompressing and expanding, 5
    definition of, 196
    descriptions of files, 122
    destination directory for, 5, 73, 122
    from file libraries, 5, 124–125, 126
    with FTP, 135–136
    Parental Controls for, 22
    preferences for, 5
    of saved text from windows, 129
    viruses in, 134
    from Web sites, warnings for, 6

downloading newsgroup postings, 73, 142–143
Driving Today keyword, 186
drop-down list, BP-4, BP-5

E

EA Games, 188
EA Lounge, 180
EA Sports, 188
Easy Designer, 150, 177
Easy Designer keyword, 150
education, online areas about, 179, 180, 192–193
eGroups, 138
Electronic Arts Platinum Service, 188
e-mail. *See also* **mailing lists**
    accessing by phone, 154
    accessing through the Internet, 162–163
    attachments to. *See* attachments
    closing automatically after sending, 7
    confirming that it was sent, 7
    definition of, 196
    deleting messages, 77–78, 90
    downloading with Automatic AOL, 4, 72
    enabling/disabling sounds for, 9
    etiquette guidelines for, 80
    Favorite Places in, 82–83, 89–90
    in Filing Cabinet. *See* Filing Cabinet
    formatting for, 5, 82–83, 94
    graphics in, 82
    list of features for, BP-13
    news delivererd to, 17–18
    number of days kept online, 7
    in Online Mailbox. *See* Online Mailbox
    Parental Controls for, 21–22
    preferences for, 7
    reading, 84–85
    receiving inappropriate e-mail, 84–85
    receiving notification of Buddy Albums, 111, 113
    receiving notification of pictures, 112
    receiving Official AOL Mail, 85
    replying to, 86–87
    replying to discussion board messages, 105
    replying to newsgroup messages, 144
    returned as undeliverable, 77
    saving, 87
    sending automatically, 4, 72
    sending carbon copies, 75–76
    sending from Address Book, 94
    sending from Member Profile, 48
    sending greeting card in, 87–88
    sending to AOL members, 88
    sending to Buddies, 60
    sending to multiple addresses, 88, 94
    sending to people on Internet, 89, 134

    signature file for, 76–77, 78–79
    sorting, 90
    status of sent mail, 74–75
    undeleting, 90
    unsending, 91
    writing, 92–93, 93–94
e-mail address
    auto-suggesting from Address Book, 7, 94
    for the Internet, 80, 92
    storing. *See* Address Book
emoticons
    avoiding in formal e-mail messages, 80
    definition of, 41, 199
    entering in chat rooms, 38
    entering in Instant Messages, 60, 65
    list of, 80–81
emphasizing text. *See* **formatting**
Enter Password box, BP-7
Entertainment channel, 177, 187–188
etiquette, 38, 50–51, 80
Evening Essentials keyword, 178
event arenas, 38–39
Event Directory, 16
event transcripts, 42
Excite search system, 147
! (exclamation point), 38
EXE files, 196
Exit option, File menu, BP-11
Explore keyword, 179

F

families. *See* **children; Parental Controls**
Favorite Places. *See also* **HotKeys list; My Places**
    adding to, 26, 152, 175
    author's Favorite Places, 176–184
    deleting items from, 29–30
    description of, 30, 196
    going to a Favorite Place, 32–33
    inserting in e-mail, 82–83, 89–90
    inserting in Instant Messages, 54–55
    modifying items and folders in, 28–29
    organizing with folders, 33–34
    storing newsgroups in, 143–144
Favorite Places icon, 26, 30, 55, 83, 89–90
Favorite Places option, Favorites menu, 28, 29, 32, 33
Favorites menu (on toolbar), BP-6
    Favorite Places option, 28, 29, 32–33. *See also* Favorite Places
    Go To Keyword option, 36. *See also* keywords
    My Hot Keys option, 27. *See also* HotKeys list
fields. *See* **text boxes**
file libraries
    downloading files from, 5, 124–125, 126
    searching, 126

of software, 147–148, 187
uploading files to, 129–131
File menu
Download Manager option, 122, 123, 196. *See also* Download Manager
Exit option, BP-11
Log Manager option, BP-11, 127
File Transfer Protocol. *See* **FTP**
files. *See also* **file libraries**
attached to e-mail messages. *See* attachments
cookies, 196
decompressing and expanding, 5
downloading. *See* downloading files
EXE files, 196
inserting in e-mail messages, 82
uploading to AOL, 129–131
viruses in, 123
Filing Cabinet
confirm before deleting files in, 5
creating new folders in, 87
downloading e-mail to Incoming Mail folder, 72
downloading postings to Incoming Postings folder, 73, 142–143
preferences for, 5, 171
reading e-mail messages in, 84
reading newsgroup messages in, 143
reducing size of, 170–171
saving e-mail messages in, 87
sending mail in Mail Waiting to Be Sent folder, 72
sending postings in Postings Waiting to be Sent folder, 73
Filing Cabinet option, Mail menu, 84, 170–171
finances, online areas about, 192
Find a Chat option, People menu, 42. *See also* **chat room**
folders
creating in Filing Cabinet, 87
Download folder, 5, 73, 122
in Favorite Places, 28–29, 33–34
general Mail folder, 87
History folder, 6
Incoming Postings folder, 73
Incoming/Saved Mail folder, 72, 84, 87
Mail Waiting to Be Sent folder, 72
Mail You've Sent folder, 87
Postings Waiting to be Sent folder, 73
for sound files, 47
font
in chat rooms, 5, 38
in e-mail messages, 5, 82
in Instant Messages, 5, 60
Font, Text & Graphics preferences, 5–6
food, online areas about, 179, 189

Food keyword, 179
formatting
in chat rooms, 5, 38, 48
for e-mail messages, 5, 82–83
for Instant Messages, 5, 60
forum, online. *See* **discussion boards**
Forward button, on browser bar, 149
free area, 196. *See also* **offline activities**
FTP (File Transfer Protocol)
description of, 134, 196
downloading files with, 135–136
uploading files to FTP sites, 136–137
using a specific FTP site, 137–138
FTP keyword, 134

G

games, 48, 49, 177, 180, 188
Games channel, 188
Games keyword, 180
Get AOL Member Profile option, People menu, 47, 49. *See also* **Member Profile**
Get Help Now keyword, BP-10, 172, 187
Go Network search system, 147
Go To Keyword option, Favorites menu, 36. *See also* **keywords**
Google search system, 147
Gopher, 147
grammar and spell checking, 9
graphics. *See also* **pictures**
compressing when loading, 7
inserting in e-mail messages, 82–83
maximum disk space used for, 6
printing, 128
greeting card, sending, 87–88
groups. *See also* **Groups@AOL; newsgroups**
in Address Book, 68–69, 70
in Buddy List, 56, 59–60
Yahoo! Groups, 138
Groups keyword, 97, 99, 197
Groups@AOL
creating private discussion areas, 97–99
creating public discussion areas, 99–100
description of, 101, 197
from groups in Address Book, 69
guidelines for, 98, 100
inviting friends to a discussion area, 101–102
joining a private discussion area, 98, 102
guest, signing on as, 163–164
Guest screen name, 163

H

harassment. *See* **offensive behavior**
headlines, reading. *See* **news**
Health channel, 188–189
heart icon. *See* **Favorite Places icon**

help. *See also* **problems, solving; reporting problems or violations**
   about AOL, BP-7, BP-10, 166–167
   in chat rooms, 44
   about computers, BP-10, 172, 187
   from other members, 169–170
Help Community keyword, 169–170
Help keyword, BP-10, 166–167
history, online areas about, 180, 183, 184
History folder, 6, 9
History keyword, 180
home page
   creating, 14, 149–150, 177
   member home pages, 152, 176
   specifying in preferences, 6
   uploading to AOL Hometown, 14, 152
   viewing Buddy's home page, 60
Homeschooling keyword, 180
Hometown, AOL, 14, 152, 176, 195
Hometown keyword, 14, 176, 195
host not responding, 172–173
hotel, connecting to AOL from, 155
HotKeys list, 27–28. *See also* **Favorite Places; My Places**
hourly rate plan. *See* **measured service**
House & Home channel, 189
HTML, definition of, 197
hyperlink. *See* **links**

I

icons
   America Online, BP-7
   AOL tray icon, 167–168, 171
   for discussion boards, 101
   disk icon, 85
   displaying emotions. *See* emoticons
   for Favorite Places, 26, 30, 55, 83, 89–90
   for Instant Messages, 66
   for messages in discussion boards, 96
IE (Internet Explorer), 151
ignoring chat room participants, 51
IM. *See* **Instant Messages**
IM button, BP-6. *See also* **Instant Messages**
Improve Yourself keyword, 187
Incoming Mail folder, 72
Incoming Postings folder, 73
Incoming/Saved Mail folder, 84, 87
Instant Messages (IMs)
   adding another Buddy to, 59
   adding emoticons to, 60, 65
   adding links to, 54–55
   auto-suggesting screen names for, 65–66
   credit card requests in, 62–63
   description of, 61, 197
   enabling/disabling sounds for, 9

   formatting for, 5, 60
   icons for, 66
   logging for, 126–128
   Parental Controls for, 22
   password requests in, 62–63
   privacy preferences for, 9, 65–66
   receiving and responding to, 61–62
   reporting problems during, 62–63
   responding with Away Message, 56–57
   sending, 60, 65
   timestamp for, 65
   viewing Buddy's profile during, 61
Instant Messenger keyword, 197
International Access keyword, 155, 158, 195
International channel, 189–190
International keyword, 181
international travel, 155, 156
Internet
   connection, problems with, 173–174
   definition of, 197
   mail gateway, 134
   Parental Controls for, 19, 22
   preferences for, 6–7
   searching. *See* searching
   signing on to AOL from, 162–163
Internet button, BP-6. *See also* **Internet**
Internet e-mail address, 80, 89, 92
Internet Explorer (Microsoft), 151, 197
Internet option, Services menu, 139–140
Internet Radio keyword, 191, 197. *See also* **Radio keyword**
Internet Relay Chat (IRC), 147
Internet Service Provider (ISP), 4, 198
italic text. *See* **formatting**
item list, BP-4, BP-5

J

jobs, online areas about, 186–187
junk mail
   fake return addresses for, 77
   from mailing lists, 138–139
   restricting, 7–8
justification of text. *See* **formatting**

K

Ka Ching keyword, 182
Kaufeld, John
   America Online 7.0 For Dummies, 4, 14, 27, 64, 124, 150
keyboard shortcuts
   adding to HotKeys list, 27–28
   to cycle through open windows, 32
   for Keyword window, BP-9, 32, 37
   for toolbar buttons, BP-6–BP-7

keyboard shorthand. *See* shorthand
Keyword button, BP-8. *See also* keywords
Keyword keyword, 31
keywords. *See also specific keywords*
    creating HotKeys for, 27
    definition of, 198
    getting a list of, 31–32
    locating for a window, 34
    using, BP-8, 36
Kids Only channel, 190
Kids Only Parental Control, 19

L

Learning Network keyword, 179, 192
Leatherman tool, 155
left justification of text. *See* formatting
library, file. *See* file libraries
links
    adding to e-mail, 82–83, 89–90
    adding to Instant Messages, 54–55
    colors of, customizing, 6
    in Web pages, 148
local access numbers, 160–162
Local Guide channel, 16, 190–191
Locate Member Online option, People menu, 45, 46
locating members, 44–45, 46, 48
location, dial-up. *See also* access numbers
    changing, 154
    creating, 155–158, 158–160
    deleting, 160
    description of, 162
Log Manager option, File menu, BP-11, 127
Logs, BP-11, 126–128
lost carrier, 173–174
lurking, 48, 198

M

mail (electronic). *See* e-mail
mail (U.S. postal service), restricting, 7–8
Mail menu (on toolbar)
    Address Book option, 68. *See also* Address Book
    Automatic AOL option, 91, 142–143. *See also* Automatic AOL
    description of, BP-6
    Filing Cabinet option, 84, 170–171. *See also* Filing Cabinet
    Mail Signatures option, 76, 78. *See also* signature file
    Read Mail option, 74. *See also* e-mail
    Recently Deleted Mail option, 90. *See also* e-mail
    Write Mail option, 70, 92–93. *See also* e-mail

Mail Signatures option, Mail menu, 76, 78. *See also* signature file
Mail Waiting to Be Sent folder, 72
Mail You've Sent folder, 87
mailbox. *See* Online Mailbox
mailing lists, 138–139, 198
Marketing preferences, 7–8
Marketing Prefs keyword, 8
master screen name, 10, 11, 22, 198
mating plug, 155
Mature Teen Parental Control, 19
measured service, 168, 176–177, 196. *See also* offline activities
media player, choosing, 8
member chat room, 38, 39–40, 42
Member Directory, 46, 63–64
Member Directory keyword, 63
Member Directory option, People menu, 63
member list, in chat room, alphabetizing, 5
Member Profile
    accessing through Member Directory, 46, 63–64
    creating, 13–14, 41, 50
    for Groups@AOL, 98
    reading, 47–48, 49, 60, 61
menu bar, 198. *See also specific menus*; toolbar
message boards. *See* discussion boards
messages. *See* discussion boards; e-mail; newsgroups
Microsoft Internet Explorer, 151, 197
mirror access, 135
modem, 154, 172–173, 198
MomsOnline keyword, 182
Motley Fool keyword, 192
mouse pointer, changing over links, 148
moving, changing location when, 154
MSIE, 151, 197
multimedia preferences, 8
music
    CD player, setting default, 8
    Entertainment channel, 187–188
    Internet Radio keyword, 191, 197
    Music channel, 191
    music events in Event Directory, 16
    Radio button, on toolbar, BP-7, 182
    Radio keyword, 182
    Teens channel, 193
Music channel, 191
My Calendar, 14–17, 195
My Favorites button, BP-3, BP-7. *See also* Favorite Places
My FTP Space keyword, 137
My Groups keyword, 98, 102
My Hot Keys option, Favorites menu, 27. *See also* HotKeys list

My News, 2, 17–18, 181, 191, 198
My Places, BP-3, BP-9, 34–35. *See also*
  Favorite Places; HotKeys list

N

Netscape keyword, 152
Netscape Navigator, 151–152
New keyword, 183
The New York Times, 181–182
news
  delivered to e-mail box. *See* My News
  Evening Essentials keyword, 178
  list of features for, BP-12
  News channel, BP-12, 191
  newsgroups about, 139
  Times keyword, 181–182
  Where Were You When keyword, 183
News channel, BP-12, 191
News keyword, BP-12
newsgroups
  browsing through lists of, 146
  description of, 139, 199
  getting and sending postings automatically, 4, 73
  Parental Controls for, 22
  posting messages to, 140
  reading messages, 140–141, 141–143
  reading messages without subscribing, 145
  replying to messages, 144
  searching for topic in, 145–146
  storing in Favorite Places, 143–144
  subscribing to, 144–145, 146
  topic hierarchies for, 139
  unsubscribing from, 146–147
Newsgroups keyword, 139, 141, 199
Newspapers keyword, BP-12
Notify AOL button
  in chat rooms, 44, 50, 51–52
  in Instant Messages, 62–63
  in Online Mailbox, 84–85
Notify AOL keyword, 50, 63, 182
NYT keyword, BP-12

O

O2 Simplify keyword, 182
offensive behavior
  in chat rooms, 44, 50, 51–52
  in e-mail messages, 84–85
  in Instant Messages, 62–63
Official AOL Mail, 85
offline, definition of, 199
offline activities. *See also* free area
  changing a dial-up location, 154–155
  creating a new dial-up location, 155–158, 158–160

  finding local access numbers, 160–162
  reading e-mail messages, 84
  reading newsgroup messages, 141–143
  setting preferences, 3–9
  writing e-mail message, 92–93
online, definition of, 199
online areas
  exploring randomly, 179
  finding. *See* AOL Search; channels; keywords
  new, 183
  remembering. *See* Favorite Places; HotKeys list; My Places
online art. *See* graphics
Online Campus keyword, 187
online forum. *See* discussion boards
online Group. *See* Groups@AOL
Online Mailbox. *See also* e-mail
  deleting messages from, 77–78
  reading messages in, 84–85
  saving messages to Filing Cabinet, 87
  sorting e-mail messages in, 90

P

PAML, 138
paranormal, online area about, 177–178
ParaScope keyword, 177–178
Parent Soup keyword, 192
Parent Time keyword, 192
Parental Controls
  age-based controls for, 19–20
  custom controls for, 21–22
  general controls for, 19–20
  screen names with permission for, 10
  selecting for screen name, 11–12
Parental Controls keyword, 20
Parental Controls option, Settings menu, 20
( ) (parentheses), 75
parenting. *See* children; Parental Controls
Parenting channel, 191–192
password
  automatically filled in, 8–9
  changing, 2–3
  choosing, 2, 10–11
  entering when signing on, BP-7
  requested by e-mail message, 84–85
  requested by Instant Message, 62–63
  storing for Automatic AOL, 74
Password keyword, 2–3
PDA keyword, 187
People Connection, 38, 43, 46, 96
People Games keyword, 48
People Here list, in chat room, 51
People menu (on toolbar), BP-6
  Chat option, 46. *See also* chat room
  Find a Chat option, 42. *See also* chat room

Get AOL Member Profile option, 47, 49. *See also* Member Profile
Locate Member Online option, 45, 46
Member Directory option, 63. *See also* Member Directory
Send Instant Message option, 65. *See also* Instant Messages
Start Your Own Chat option, 39–40, 45. *See also* chat room
Personal Filing Cabinet. *See* Filing Cabinet
Personal Finance channel, 192
phone. *See* telephone
phone numbers. *See* telephone numbers
pictures. *See also* graphics
   albums for. *See* albums
   captions for, 110
   developing, 112–113
   digital, uploading, 117–119
   e-mail notification of, 85, 112
   expiration time for, 113, 115
   Parental Controls for, 22
   saving online, 113, 115
   sharing, 113
   viewing, 113
Pictures keyword, **108, 109, 111, 112, 114, 117, 200**
PKZIP, 200
Platinum Service, 188
player, media, choosing, 8
pointer, changing over links, 148
Pop-up windows, advertising from, 8
postal service mail. *See* mail (U.S. postal service)
Postings Waiting to be Sent folder, 73
preferences
   AOL as default Internet application, 4
   Automatic AOL, 4
   Buddy Lists, 65–66
   chat room, 5
   discussion boards, 103–104
   downloads, 5, 129
   e-mail, 7
   Filing Cabinet, 5, 171
   fonts, 5–6
   graphics, 5–6
   Instant Messages, 65–66
   Internet, 6–7
   marketing, 7–8
   multimedia, 8
   password, 8–9
   privacy, 9, 65–66
   setting, 3–4
   sounds, 9
   spell and grammar checking, 9
   toolbar, 9

Preferences keyword, **3, 171**
Preferences option, Settings menu, 3
Premium Services
   Games, 177, 188
   Parental Controls for, 19, 21, 22
presentations, given in chat rooms, 38
primary screen name, **10, 199**
Print Central keyword, 187
Print menu, Print option, 128
Privacy preferences, 9, 65–66
Private Chat keyword, 40
private chat room, 38–39, 40, 45, 57–59
private discussion area, 97–99, 102
problems, solving. *See also* help; reporting problems or violations
   billing problems, 168
   Filing Cabinet too full, 170–171
   host not responding, 172–173
   HotKeys not working, 28
   locating lost windows, 169
   lost carrier, 173–174
   low resources, 170–171
   purging browser cache, 171
   signing on failures, BP-8
   TCP/IP lost connection, 173–174
   technical support phone numbers, 169
   using AOL tray icon for, 167–168
   Web pages not loading, 174
Profile keyword, **13, 41, 199**
profiles, 199. *See also* Member Profile; My News
protocol, 38, 50–51, 80
public discussion area, 99–100
public rooms, 38, 42
publications, about America Online, 4
Publicly Accessible Mailing Lists, 138

Q

? (question mark), 38
Quotes button, BP-7. *See also* stock information

R

Radio button (on AOL toolbar), BP-7, 182
radio buttons (in dialog boxes), BP-5
Radio keyword, 182. *See also* Internet Radio keyword
Radio@AOL, 182
Read button, BP-2, BP-6. *See also* e-mail
Read Mail option, Mail menu, 74. *See also* e-mail
Recently Deleted Mail option, Mail menu, 90. *See also* e-mail
recipes, online area about, 179, 189

recreation, newsgroups about, 139
reference information, online area about, 192–193
Reload button, on browser bar, 149
reporting problems or violations. *See also* problems, solving
  in chat rooms, 44, 50, 51–52
  in e-mail messages, 84–85
  in Instant Messages, 62–63
  technical support phone numbers, 169
Research & Learn channel, 192–193
Research a Company keyword, 187. *See also* Company Research keyword
researching topics. *See* searching
resources, low, 170–171
Resources & Tips keyword, 194
Restricted Sites, 6
right justification of text. *See* formatting
right-clicking, 48, 82–83, 94
Roadandtrack keyword, 186
role-playing chat rooms, 48–49
//roll comand in chat rooms, 49
Rotunda, 39

S

{S command for playing sounds, 47
Salary and Benefits keyword, 186–187
sales staff phone number, 169
scammer, definition of, 199
scheduling appointments. *See* My Calendar
science, newsgroups about, 139
Science keyword, 183
screen name
  creating, 10–12
  definition of, 199
  deleting, 12
  Guest screen name, 163
  restoring after deleting, 22–23
  selecting when signing on, BP-7
  types of, 10
Screen Names keyword, 10, 12
Search keyword, 147
search systems, 147
searching
  America Online and the Internet, BP-14, 30, 147
  file libraries, 126
  Member Directory, 63–64
  for newsgroup topics, 145–146
secondary screen name, 10, 12
security preferences, 6
Select Location box, BP-7
Select Screen Name box, BP-7
Send Instant Message option, People menu, 65. *See also* Instant Messages

Services menu (on toolbar)
  description of, BP-6
  Internet option, 139–140
Session Log, BP-11, 126–128
Settings menu (on toolbar)
  description of, BP-6
  Parental Controls option, 20. *See also* Parental Controls
  Preferences option, 3. *See also* preferences
Setup window
  Add Location button, 155–158
  Add Number button, 160–162
  for Automatic AOL, 72–74
  for Buddy List, 9, 54, 56, 59–60, 65–66
  Expert Setup button, 154, 158–160, 173
Shop button, BP-6
Shopping Assistant, preferences for, 7
Shopping channel, 193
shortcut keys. *See* keyboard shortcuts
shorthand
  avoiding in formal e-mail messages, 80
  in chat rooms, 38, 42
  list of abbreviations for, 81
  in role-playing chat rooms, 48–49
Sign Off menu, Sign Off option, BP-11
signature file
  appending to e-mail, 78–79, 82
  creating or editing, 76–77
  default signature file, 78
  description of, 91–92
signing off America Online, BP-11
signing on to America Online
  from another computer (as a Guest), 163–164
  through the Internet, 162–163
  in Sign On window, BP-7–BP-8
smiley button, 38, 60
smilies, 199. *See also* emoticons
snail mail. *See* mail (U.S. postal service)
sociology, newsgroups about, 139
software. *See also* file libraries
  at Computer Center channel, 187
  Winsock applications, 147–148
solving problems. *See* problems, solving
sounds
  in Buddy List, 65
  in chat room, 5, 47
  folders for, 47
  preferences for, 9
spam, reporting to AOL, 84–85
spell checking, 9, 48, 82
splitter, 155
sports, online areas about, 184, 193
Sports channel, 193
Sports Community keyword, 193

sports events, in Event Directory, 16
Start Your Own Chat option, People menu,
   39–40, 45. *See also* chat room
starting America Online. *See* signing on to
   America Online
StartUp keyword, 187
stock information, BP-7, 16, 192
Stop button, on browser bar, 149
stopping America Online, BP-11
Suggestions keyword, 166
support phone number, BP-8, 169
swearing. *See* offensive behavior
system information for computer, 167–168
system status of AOL, 167
system tray, 167
system-wide chat rooms, 42

T

tabs, BP-4, BP-5
Talk newsgroup topics, 139
taskbar, Windows, 167
TCP/IP lost connection, 173–174
teaching, online areas about, 179, 180,
   192–193
teams. *See* sports, online areas about
technical support phone number, BP-8, 169
technology, online area about, 178
Teens channel, 193
telephone
   accessing e-mail by, 154
   restricting advertising from, 8
telephone cords, 155
telephone jack converter, 155
telephone line, problems with, 172–173
telephone numbers
   for AOLNet, 155
   storing. *See* Address Book
   technical support, BP-8, 169
Telephone Preference Service, 8
Telnet, 147
Terms of Service (TOS)
   listing rules with TOS keyword, 51
   not applying to newsgroups, 139
   reporting violations of. *See* reporting problems
      or violations
text boxes, BP-4, BP-5
text color. *See* formatting
text font. *See* font
text size. *See* formatting
Time keyword, BP-12
Times keyword, 181–182
title bar, BP-4, BP-5

toolbar. *See also* menu bar; *specific menus
   and buttons*
   buttons on, BP-6–BP-7
   customizing, 9
   definition of, 200
Tools & Reference keyword, 187
TOS. *See* Terms of Service
TOS keyword, listing Terms of Service
   rules, 51
tracking. *See* Logs
transcripts from AOL Live chats, 42
Travel channel, 194
traveling. *See also* international travel
   accessing e-mail by phone, 154
   connecting to AOL from a hotel, 155
   connection tools for, 155
   creating a dial-up location for, 155–158
   international, 155, 156
   signing on through the Internet, 162–163
   Travel channel, 194
tray icon for AOL, 167–168, 171
troubleshooting. *See* problems, solving
Trusted Sites, 6
TTY support phone number, 169
type size. *See* formatting
typeface. *See* font

U

UFOs, online area about, 177–178
underlined text
   in chat rooms, e-mail, and Instant Messages.
      See formatting
   in Web pages (links). *See* links
unlimited usage plan, 176
Upload keyword, 131
uploading files
   to AOL, 129–131
   to AOL Hometown, 14, 152
   of digital photos, 117–119
   to FTP sites, 136–137
   to private Web space on AOL, 137
U.S. postal service mail. *See* mail (U.S.
   postal service)

V

violations, reporting. *See* reporting
   problems or violations
Virus keyword, 134
virus-checking software, 134
viruses, in downloaded files, 123, 134
voltage transformer, 155
vulgarity. *See* offensive behavior

W

.WAV files, playing in chat room, 47
weather forecast, in My Calendar, 14
Weather keyword, 194
Web. *See* World Wide Web
Web browsers, 148–149, 151–152
Web page, personal. *See* home page
Web Page keyword, 177
Web sites. *See also* home page
  America Online, 163
  for American Greetings, 87–88
  browsing, 148–149, 150–151
  downloading files from, 6
  heart icon in, 89–90
  not loading, 174
  remembering. *See* Favorite Places; HotKeys list;
    My Places
  Restricted Sites, 6
  searching for, BP-14, 30, 147
  Trusted Sites, 6
  for Yahoo! Groups, 138
  for You've Got Pictures, 114
Webcrawler search system, 147
Welcome channel, 186
Welcome window, diagram of, BP-2–BP-3
Where Were You When keyword, 183
Who Am I keyword, 184
Window menu, 31
windows. *See also* dialog boxes
  locating, 31, 169
  printing contents of, 128
  saving text from, 128–129
Windows taskbar, 167
Winsock applications, 200
Winsock applications, support for, 147–148

WinZip keyword, 131
WinZip software, 131, 200
women, online areas for, 182, 194
Women channel, 194
Women's Activities keyword, 194
Women's Features keyword, 194
World News keyword, BP-12
World Wide Web, 200. *See also* Internet;
  Web sites
Write button, BP-2, BP-6. *See also* e-mail
Write Mail option, Mail menu, 70, 92–93.
  See also e-mail
WWW preferences, 6–7

Y

Yahoo! Groups Web site, 138
Yahoo! search system, 147
Young Teen Parental Control, 19
You've Got Mail announcement, 84
You've Got Mail button, BP-2
You've Got Pictures. *See also* albums;
  pictures
  description of, 119, 200
  developing pictures, 112–113
  with digital photos, 117–119
  saving pictures online, 115
  Web site, 114
You've Got Pictures button, BP-2

Z

ZIP files, 5, 131, 200